THE SOCIAL JUSTICE AGENDA:
JUSTICE, ECOLOGY, POWER AND THE CHURCH

THE
SOCIAL JUSTICE
AGENDA

Justice, Ecology, Power and the Church

DONAL DORR

ORBIS BOOKS
Maryknoll, New York 10545

Published in Ireland by
Gill and Macmillan Ltd
Goldenbridge
Dublin 8
and in the United States by
Orbis Books, Maryknoll
New York 10545
© Donal Dorr 1991
Printed in England
All rights reserved.

ISBN 0 88344 722 3 (Orbis Books)

Library of Congress Cataloging in Publication Data
Dorr, Donal.
Social justice agenda : justice, ecology, power, and the church / Donal Dorr
p.   cm.
Includes bibliographical references and index.
ISBN 0-88344-722-3 (pbk.) : $9.95
1. Christianity and justice—Catholic Church.
2. Catholic Church—Doctrines. 3. Social justice. I Title
BX1795.J87D87 1991
261.8–dc20   90-49049
CIP

Contents

Introduction

THIS BOOK is an attempt to meet the need for a general and fairly simple introduction to the topic of justice-and-peace as it has emerged for the Christian Churches in recent years. It takes its origin from a talk I was asked to give in Rome four years ago under the title, 'The Church's Teaching on Justice and Peace, Twenty Years after Vatican II'. The discussion afterwards, and later contact with many people interested in these issues, made me aware of the need for a more extended treatment of the subject. Over the past four years I have continued to work on the topics covered in my talk and the material has gradually expanded so that it now forms the main part of this book. I have, however, widened the question so that the book deals not only with the *teaching* of the Churches but also with the kind of *action* that needs to be undertaken by them.

There have been major developments in the spirituality, theology and teaching of the Churches on social issues over the past generation. These changes have come so quickly that even very committed Christians have found it difficult to keep up with them. My hope is that the book will be useful to individuals or study groups who would like an introductory study of these developments.

The emphasis here is on the role that can be played by *the institutional Church* in responding to social justice issues. In this sense the book is intended to be complementary to another that I published last year, entitled *Integral Spirituality* in which I was concerned with what can be done by individual Christians and by small committed groups. In the present book I am addressing the question of the role of the official Church and Church leaders—their teaching and their action.

The book is divided into three parts. In the first part my aim is to give a general account of the major issues of social justice which confront the Christian today. This is my attempt to paint the broad picture. I give an outline of fourteen topics which, as I see it, constitute the present social justice agenda of the main

1

Churches. These topics range from the gap between rich and poor to justice for women, and from the struggle for human rights to the issue of justice within the Church.

In the second part of the book I go on to give some account of what the Churches have to say about these issues. I begin this part by tracing the historical development of the social justice agenda both in the Roman Catholic Church (chapter 2) and in the World Council of Churches (chapter 3). I believe it is necessary for Christians in each of the major traditions to be aware not only of what has been going on in their own Church but also of the developments in *other* traditions. This is especially helpful at the present time because the different Christian traditions are obviously converging in a very fruitful way. I feel it is important to provide the historical background to the present stance of the Churches on social issues. This can be a great help to the many committed Christians of the present generation who were educated into an older and more private style of spirituality. An awareness of the way Church teaching has developed over the years can lessen the sense of confusion often experienced by such people. It challenges and supports them as they face up to the very radical shift of emphasis in the spirituality to which all of us are now being called.

In chapter 4 I spell out in a very concrete way the main principles or guidelines of Christian teaching on issues of justice and peace. This seems to me to be necessary because in recent years there has been a lot of uncertainty on these matters even among those who are most committed to living out an authentic spirituality. Much of this uncertainty arises from the fact that the present teaching of the Churches on some issues has moved on a long way from what Church leaders were teaching a generation ago; indeed it may seem that on some issues the Church has made a U-turn in its teaching—and quite a lot of committed Christians (and even some Church leaders) are not aware of the changes. In an effort to bring some clarity and to help people to update themselves I have picked out a number of key principles. Taking each in turn I have set down a summary of the Church teaching of a generation ago on this point; then I have given a summary of what I understand to be the current teaching on the same issue; and in a short commentary I have tried to bring out both the continuity and the contrast between the two.

2

I believe it is not enough to look at the agenda and examine what the Church has to *say* about the various issues of social justice. There is a further vital question of what the individual Christian and the Church as a whole can *do*. So, in the third part of this book, I explore various ways in which Christians and the Churches can commit themselves to the promotion of justice both in society and in the Church itself.

I cover four main topics in this third part of the book. Firstly, (in chapter 5) I try to clarify what it means for the Church itself to be in solidarity with the poor and to make an option for the poor. In this context I discuss the importance of engaging in a social analysis of the structures of society—and of the role of the institutional Church in society. I then go on to offer some suggestions about how the Church can challenge the various kinds of injustice outlined in the first chapter.

Next I go on (in chapter 6) to examine the crucial contribution which can be made by Christians and the Churches to the search for alternatives, that is towards the building of a society and a world that is more just, more respectful of the Earth, more sustainable and more participative.

In the last two chapters of the book I concentrate on what is involved in the Church itself becoming more just. The key issue here is that the Church has power of various kinds and so we have to examine how this power is to be used in ways that are truly just.

I devote chapter 7 to showing that the ability to do theology is itself a power—a power that can be used either to dominate people or to liberate them. The whole Christian community, and each individual Christian, is called and privileged to engage in a theological exploration of the faith we live by. If the Church is to be just it must ensure that its theological power is not used to oppress ordinary people but to set them free. I then suggest that there is need for major changes in theological institutes if they are to serve the Christian community as they ought. Those who own them and those who teach in them are called to make 'an option for the poor'—for the 'common people'—who are hungry for help in articulating their faith and their spirituality.

In the final chapter I take up an issue that is closely related to the previous one. This time, however, the topic is not just theology but the wider question of 'formation' and the training for various kinds of special ministry in the Church—for lay leadership, for membership of a religious community, and for the priesthood. What type of formation is required if the Christian Churches are to give a central role to justice? I examine different models of formation and explore ways in which commitment to the transformation of society and practical experience of community-building may be integrated with other aspects of formation.

I am grateful to the Irish Missionary Union (IMU) which has sponsored the writing of this book. The book is directed to a wide audience of committed Church people, but I hope it will find a particular resonance in the lives of some of the thousands of missionaries all over the world who are linked to the IMU. I am particularly indebted to my sister, Ben Kimmerling, for her patient and perceptive criticism of various drafts of the material and for suggesting improvements in both context and style. I wish also to thank Bridget Lunn for her editorial work and her work on the index.

Donal Dorr, Easter 1990

4

PART ONE
The Present Agenda

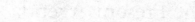

1

Major Issues of Social
Justice

THERE ARE a number of major issues which, taken together,
make up what may be called 'The Social Justice Agenda'.
I propose here to give an outline of these central themes of
Christian social concern today. As I work through the various
items on the agenda it will become clear that some of them are
closely linked to others. It will also be obvious that some are
more fundamental that others. However, I am not concerned
here with establishing any order of priority but only with intro-
ducing the major areas of concern.

1. The Gap

The most obvious item on the social justice agenda is the
very wide gap between the rich and the poor. This gap exists at
various levels:

—In most cities, towns and rural areas there are some individuals or families whose income is ten or twenty times that of
many of their neighbours.

—Within most countries there is a wide gulf between different
social classes; and this class distinction is based mainly on wealth.

—In the world as a whole there is a huge gap in the standard of
living between the rich countries (often called 'the developed
countries' or, more recently, 'the North') and the poor countries
(called 'less developed' or 'developing' or 'the South'). It is true
that in almost every poor country there is a very small percentage
of extremely wealthy people; but this only makes the poverty of
the country as a whole more striking.

—Finally, there is, on the whole, a widening gap between able-
bodied adults and many categories of people who are in a vulnerable situation, e.g. the sick, the old, those who are mentally
ill or handicapped. These groups of people are 'poor' in the

particular sense that they are in a position of being dependent on others. And their dependence gives rise to a further type of poverty in their close relatives who often find themselves weighed down for years on end with the burden of caring for them without adequate support from the community or the State. Because of the advances in science and technology, dependent people, and those who care for them, now have the possibility of living a much more fulfilled life than in the past. But, sadly, very many of them are deprived of these benefits because most of the available resources go to healthy adults.

The mere fact that some people are more wealthy than others is not, in itself, a social injustice. But the existence of gross poverty alongside conspicuous wealth is morally unacceptable. The fact that in our world millions of people do not have the basic necessities of life while others live in luxury is a basic injustice: it infringes the most fundamental human right of all— the right to life. The Christian tradition maintains that the goods of the Earth are there for the welfare of all the Earth's inhabitants— and that the right to private property takes second place to this.

Are the rich responsible for keeping the poor poor? On the whole, yes. Wealthy individuals and nations cannot disclaim responsibility for the persistence of poverty. Not, of course, that they normally set out consciously to deprive others. But power goes hand-in-hand with wealth and, by and large, the wealthy use their power to block the kind of changes that would make it possible to overcome major poverty.

There is only one way in which major poverty problems can be eliminated or minimised. That is by making better use of the available resources. This is not simply a matter of redistributing the money and goods of the wealthy; for they would have to be shared among so may people that they would not go very far in alleviating poverty. What is required, rather, is that the energy, the raw materials and the technology resources used at present to provide luxuries for the rich be redirected in such a way as to ensure that everybody on Earth could have enough to live on in frugal comfort. For instance, the resources used to buy and run private motor cars, and to build the motorways required by so many private vehicles, could be used instead to provide excellent mass transport systems (trams, trains, etc) available to all.

Again, there is sufficient arable land in the world to produce nourishing vegetable food to feed all the inhabitants of the Earth; but many go hungry because too much of this land is devoted to producing foodstuffs for cattle and pigs to provide meat for better-off people (and even for their pets). Those who are well-off and powerful are unwilling to relinquish their privileges, and so the poor remain impoverished.

Furthermore, in our world the wealth of the rich derives very largely from the fact that they are in a position to take advantage of the poor. As I have just pointed out, the disparity in wealth is closely linked to a disparity in *power*. The unfair terms of trade between rich and poor countries is a clear example of the links between wealth and power. The products produced by the poor nations (e.g. tea, coffee, cocoa, copper) are almost always sold on the world market at a price that allows them very little profit. There countries are not strong enough economically or politically to be able to ensure better prices. Any efforts they make to gear up for a 'trade war' are easily circumvented by the rich and powerful nations and the multinational companies.

It is true that in 1973–4, the oil-producing nations of OPEC won a short-term victory when they succeeded in raising the price of oil to a more reasonable level. But they have lost the long-term trade war, for the price of oil has dropped disastrously when compared to the price of goods produced in the wealthy countries. And no other group of primary-producing countries has been able to gain even the little success gained by OPEC. Those who are rich can use their wealth to gain power; and this power can be used to make them still more wealthy. They can ensure that the poor countries are competing against each other (e.g. in producing coppers, coffee or cocoa at very low prices). By building up stocks of tea, coffee, beef, copper, etc., they can protect themselves against any threat of higher prices.

It has become increasingly clear in recent years that there is no realistic possibility that the poor countries as a whole can catch up with the wealthy ones. In the first place it is now evident that there are not sufficient resources to enable the populations of the poor countries to have the kind of life-style that is considered normal in the better-off countries. This means that the notion of 'development for all' is simply an illusion (if what is in question is the wasteful Western model of development).

9

Secondly, we have now no excuse for continuing to believe that the so-called developed countries owe their development mainly to hard work, the development of technology, good planning, and a lot of productive investment. It is clear that much of what was called 'development' was actually exploitation. Firstly, it was an exploitation of natural resources, starting usually with the resources of the country that was undergoing 'development' and moving on quickly to those of 'less developed' countries. Secondly, there was the exploitation of people; here, once again, it began with the weaker sectors of the country itself and this led on to exploitation of the people of poorer countries. So the other side of the coin of 'development' of the rich countries was the misdevelopment of the poorer ones. Powerful nations took advantage of weak and poor ones either through old-style colonialism or, more recently, by imposing on them grossly unjust terms of trade.

All this raises major issues for those who wish to work for justice in the world—issues both of reparation for past wrongs and of the restructuring of present international relationships. Those of us who live in a wealthy nation or as part of the better-off class in a poor country may not be making a deliberate decision to take advantage of poorer nations and classes. But we profit from the position in which we find ourselves: our cup of tea costs us little because the tea-pickers work long hours in difficult conditions for a pitiful wage. This illustrates what is meant when people say that the problem is not simply individual *acts* of injustice but rather *structures* of injustice. If we are content to go along with the existing situation, without attempting to change the structures, then we are colluding in injustice. Many of us claim to know little or nothing about international economics or structures of injustice; but this convenient ignorance can hardly relieve us of all responsibility for the poverty and powerlessness of others which allows us to buy products at an unduly low price.

I hope I have said enough to bring out the point that the present wide gap between the rich and the poor is not merely an unfortunate fact but is also a major moral problem. Indeed it is the most obvious issue on the social justice agenda. In recent times many committed Christians, Church leaders, and theologians have come to the conclusion that the only authentic way for the Church to respond to this major problem is to make what has come to be called 'an option for the poor'. (In chapter 5 of this book I shall give an account of what is meant by such an option and in subsequent chapters I shall go on to spell out different aspects of what it involves.)

2. International Debt

A second item on the present social justice agenda is closely related to the previous one; it is international debt. Even ten years ago few would have thought that by now it would have become such a pressing issue. But now we all know that the economics of very many African and Latin American countries are utterly crushed and distorted by the burden of debt.

In order to keep up their interest payments, the governments of many of these countries have been forced to impose intolerable sacrifices on their people. Currencies have been devalued by 400–500 per cent, resulting in huge rises in the cost of living, while the income of ordinary workers has scarcely risen. For many nations the pressure to deal with their debts has wiped out any serious possibility of *genuine* development in the foreseeable future. All the resources of the government have been focussed on exporting food and other products (e.g. timber from the tropical forests or unprocessed minerals), in order to earn 'hard currency' for interest payments. Land badly needed to produce food for the ordinary inhabitants of the countries concerned has instead been given over to producing cash crops such as coffee or fruit for export. This means the abandonment of the kind of agricultural development that is designed to help peasant farmers produce food for local needs. Furthermore, money is no longer available for the development of the kind of labour-intensive industry that would provide employment for the millions of workers who have come into the cities in search of jobs. The effect of these policies is that the main burden of debt-repayment is being carried by the poorer classes in the indebted countries— the very people who, in the first place, benefited least from the loans incurred by the governments of their countries.

How did this disastrous situation come about on such a widespread scale? It was the result of the policy of the wealthy nations and their banks.[1] Fifteen years ago, the OPEC countries began to invest in Western banks the huge amounts of money

11

they had made as a result of the sudden rise in the price of oil. In order to use up this 'spare' money, the banks offered large loans, at favourable interest rates, to poor countries. These loans were used to finance utterly unrealistic 'development plans'. In fact the loans have generally been of more benefit to the donor countries than to the recipients. Much of the money was used to pay inflated prices to Western construction companies for carrying out so-called development projects. The competing companies paid large bribes to corrupt government officials— and added the cost of these bribes to their bill for the 'development' work. This bribery undermined the whole fabric of political life in many 'developing countries', and a lot of the borrowed money was siphoned off into the Swiss bank accounts of politicians.

There was little likelihood that this misguided investment in development could ever create sufficient wealth to pay back the enormous loans that had been handed out so eagerly to poorer countries. But the problem became much worse some years later when the supply of money began to dry up. At this time the banks increased the interest rates on their loans. Before long the indebted countries could not even afford to pay off the interest on their debts. So the unpaid interest was added on to the original loans. In this way a country which had borrowed $20 billion could find itself owing twice that amount—and unable to prevent the debt spiralling ever higher. So the present 'debt crisis' of the poor countries has been caused partly by the unwise development policies of their own governments but even more by the policies of Western banks.

In some cases governments are saddled with heavy debts which they themselves did not take on at all. For some of the largest loans were incurred by corrupt military regimes to finance wars of repression against the resistance forces of their own countries. When eventually these regimes were overthrown (e.g. in Nicaragua, Uganda, the Philippines) the incoming governments were forced to take on responsibility for repaying these debts!

But how can governments be forced to repay these loans? The answer shows the close link between Western privately-owned banks and Western governments. The International Monetary Fund (IMF) is a kind of international bank for governments. Its policies are determined by those who have the largest shares in it—and these are the Western banks. The IMF has imposed harsh penalties on any government which has failed to pay interest on foreign debts. Countries can be deprived of the facilities needed for foreign trade if they do not meet the demands of the IMF.

IMF policy is blatantly biased in favour of the major Western nations. When the governments of indebted countries ask for a rescheduling of their debt this is granted only on conditions laid down by the IMF. These conditions include the imposition of very harsh austerity measures, which hit the poorer people hardest of all. The IMF also insists that these countries open up their markets to imports from the West. In this way the poor countries become even more tied in to the global economic system which is dominated by the countries of 'the North'. They do not have the opportunity to try to solve their economic problems by closing themselves off from outside and using their own resources to meet the basic needs of their own people.

Even the most hard-nosed of the Western bankers have now acknowledged that it is unrealistic to expect a full repayment of loans by the very poorest countries. This is shown by the fact that many banks have been selling off their loans at a fraction of their nominal value.

When the leaders of the wealthy nations get together they propose various schemes to reduce the debt burden. But what these schemes offer is 'too little and too late'. In fact the proposals which come out of such meetings are inspired more by self-interest than by moral considerations. Widespread defaulting on debt-repayment would undermine confidence in the whole banking and financial system of the West; so it makes good economic sense to cut the losses rather than pursue impossible demands. But the issue of international debt needs to be looked at from a different perspective—from a *moral* point of view.

Many indebted countries have paid back more than sufficient to have repaid their loan in full if interest rates had not been increased. A spokesperson for Latin American and Caribbean countries says:

> If we look at it objectively, Latin America has already paid its debts. But today we still owe more than was originally contracted. Under present conditions the debt can never be paid

13

and will become a kind of 'tribute' that Latin America must pay and keep paying for life.[2]

It is socially unjust to expect poor countries to pay back up to five times the original loan when they had no effective say in determining the new interest rates. A moral assessment of all the circumstances suggests that it is no longer accurate to refer to most of these international loans as 'debts' in the normal sense of the word. It is time to cry 'halt' to repayments, or at least to scale them down very considerably. An easing of the burden of debt is one essential element in the establishment of an international order of peace and human progress based on justice.

3. Oppression and Liberation

Alongside the *economic* problem of the yawning gap between the rich and the poor there is a more obviously *political* issue: some individuals, groups, classes, races and nations are oppressing others. This oppression may take the form of colonialism, where a whole people is the victim of the imperialistic expansionism of another country. Namibia, which has been called the last of the old colonies, has now at last gained independence. But there are many other nations which are still unwillingly under the political control of more powerful neighbours; Tibet and the Baltic republics of Lithuania, Latvia and Estonia are examples currently in the news.

Oppression takes place *within* nations as well as between them. The people of many countries today are crushed down by repressive governments. These make full use of heavily armed security forces; torture and intimidation are common; and the most sophisticated technology is used to spy on anybody suspected of being subversive. In many cases these oppressive regimes are supported by the governments of one or other of the super-powers, who are protecting their own interests in the region. In all cases they are helped by being able to buy arms from dealers who are, in effect, acting as agents for the countries and companies who produce the arms for export.

In all of these countries there is some measure of resistance, some effort to achieve liberation. Such struggles for freedom give rise to major moral issues. Very frequently the moral dilemmas facing oppressed people or their friends are presented in very

14

simplistic terms. All the nuances are omitted and only one choice is presented: either to accept the authority of the government or to engage in armed resistance. It is in the interest of extremists on both sides to limit the choices in this way. But the range of options is much broader than this.

The struggle for political liberation can take many forms, ranging from guerrilla warfare to strikes, mass protests and passive resistance. In the next section I shall look at the kind of moral issues that arise in regard to these various courses of action. However, before doing so I want here to note that to be engaged in a struggle for liberation is not necessarily a matter of taking up arms against oppressive authorities.

It is no exaggeration to say that genuine political liberation cannot be achieved by military means. It is true, of course, that in some situations an armed struggle may be *necessary*—but it is certainly not *sufficient*. History shows clearly that, if a liberation movement relies mainly on military means, the results are disastrous. For even if the rebellion succeeds in toppling the oppressive regime, the new government is almost certain to be authoritarian from the beginning and to become oppressive as soon as it comes up against serious opposition. The only effective way to ensure that the struggle for freedom brings about genuine political liberation is to begin by building participative structures at every level of society. The great temptation for those who are working for liberation is to postpone this strictly political activity until there has been some success in the military struggle. But, if priority is given to military action, the whole effort is very likely to become imbued with military values:

—Decisions will be made 'from the top down' rather than based on real consensus.

—Strategies will be based on short-term advantage rather than the long-term needs of the whole community.

—Leaders will resort to authoritarian modes of ensuring cooperation instead of going through the slow and difficult process of education and animation of the community.

—Effective power will come to be held by those who have control of the guns rather than by those who can mobilise the mass of the people.

It is clear, then, that the struggle for political liberation is much broader and deeper than a purely military struggle. But the

15

notion of liberation has to be extended even further, far beyond the limits of political liberation. For instance, there are very close links between the economic sphere and the political sphere, so genuine liberation must include economic liberation. If a nation is totally dependent economically on other countries then its independence is a kind of sham and real liberation has not in fact been achieved.

This was the situation of many African countries when they first obtained political independence a generation ago. Since then the situation of most of them has become worse rather than better—and they are joined in this plight by most Latin American countries and some of the countries of Asia. What they are experiencing now is economic exploitation rather than political oppression in the strict sense. For them, 'liberation' has little to do with armed struggle or political activity in the usual sense. It has far more to do with getting out from under the burden of debt, getting a just price for the products they have to sell, being able to abandon economic policies that benefit the countries of 'the North' rather than their own people.

Another form of oppression is cultural. Minority groups in many countries of the world are treated as second-class citizens. Their languages and traditions are ignored or despised. At times this is a matter of official government policy. More commonly it arises simply through the insensitivity of governments and of the dominant political groupings whom they represent.

A particularly unfortunate kind of cultural oppression is that which is imposed on those minorities that are known as 'tribal peoples'. In various parts of Asia, in Australia, Latin America, and North America, and above all in Africa, there are many ethnic groups who still live according to the traditional or 'tribal' pattern. The way of life of these people is now at risk. More and more Third World countries have adopted either a capitalist or a Marxist version of the Western model of development. This has made it almost impossible for the tribal groups to retain their traditional pattern of life.

The threat comes from a combination of economic and cultural factors. Economically, these groups are being sucked into the unified global market which undermines many of the ways in which they supported themselves in the past. And culturally their way of life is made to seem obsolete by comparison with

16

what they hear on the radio and come in contact with through the other mass media and the schools. All over the world the traditional tribal peoples are being 'westernised' in these ways.

A small number of them adjust successfully and bring together some of the best elements of the two very different 'worlds' which they inhabit. But, in the case of the great majority, their traditional culture is, unfortunately, seriously undermined and is not replaced by any tradition which can provide them with a pattern and purpose in their lives. The result is the disinheriting of millions of people of their cultural identity. Very many of these 'lost' people become social misfits—victims of alcoholism or petty criminals. Meanwhile the world suffers an irreplaceable loss: hundreds of traditional cultures and languages, the riches of a vast variety of ways of life, are gone for ever.

No wonder, then, that many of those who are committed to full liberation for their people have come to believe that cultural liberation is not an optional 'extra' but must be at the heart of their struggle. My own experience of working to promote community leadership in several African countries confirms this view. Perhaps the greatest needs of the leaders with whom I have worked are (a) a *belief* in themselves and their own people and (b) a *motive* for being at the service of others. This is especially difficult at present when the value system being imported from the West suggests (a) that they are 'undeveloped' or backward and (b) that the way to be successful is to promote one's own self-interest.

There is a major ethical crisis in many of the so-called developing countries. It arises largely because of a loss of the traditional values.[3] In my opinion the problem cannot be solved by a more vigorous preaching of Christian or Muslim values. It is true that these world religions call for self-sacrifice and the service of others; and that they provide a basis for such values. But the message of Christianity and Islam cannot strike deep into the heart of any people unless it is related to, and even embodied in, the people's own culture and tradition. What is needed is some way of helping people to 'come home' to their traditional heritage. Once they rediscover and appreciate their own roots they have a solid basis for ethical behaviour and service of the community—a basis without which Christian or Islamic faith remains superficial. People who are rooted in their

17

own culture can evaluate that culture, preserving the best of their traditional values and correcting or adapting aspects that need further development. All this is included in genuine cultural liberation.

The question of cultural liberation also arises in the so-called developed countries when poorer classes or groups begin to struggle for their rights. Poor people everywhere tend to have a very poor self-image. They have been taught to be ashamed of their accents and customs and to undervalue their own abilities—and those of their neighbours. Anybody who seeks to promote the real liberation of the poor must address this cultural-psychological problem. In my opinion it must even take priority over other aspects of the struggle against oppression. But that does not mean that economic and political liberation must wait until the poor have learned to think well of themselves. For even relatively minor victories in the political and economic spheres can be very effective in helping the poor to overcome their poor self-image. The best strategy for would-be leaders is to work for such small but visible victories precisely in order to transform the consciousness of the people. This in turn will give them the staying-power they need to engage in the long struggle for liberation in every sphere.

4. Violence or Non-violence?

Discussion of the question of liberation leads on naturally to the next item on the social justice agenda—the question of the military and political *means* that may be used either to resist oppression or to preserve the security of the State. This is a matter of particular urgency in our world when the weapons deployed in the name of security pose a threat to all human life on the planet. In this context it is important to start with the right questions. In regard to struggles for liberation it is far more important to ask what effective *non-violent* means can be used than to ask about the conditions under which a resort to violence might be justified. And in regard to relations between the nations, it is far more urgent to ask how *disarmament* can be promoted that to ask what weapons could be used under what circumstances.

In the area of the struggle of oppressed people against tyrannical regimes in their own countries there have been remarkable

18

developments in recent years. Governments now have at their disposal such powerful and destructive weapons that armed resistance has become extremely difficult—and very costly in civilian lives. On the other hand, those who struggle against injustice have found ways of using less violent means that can be far more effective. For instance, international sanctions helped in the overthrow of the oppressive Rhodesian regime and are putting pressure on the present South African government. Internally, a major role in the downfall of the repressive Argentinean regime was played by the regular weekly protests of mothers of those who had 'disappeared'. In recent times in country after country, from the Philippines to Eastern Europe, mass demonstrations and other forms of 'people power' were an effective instrument of radical change. (There have been failures too; for instance, resistance in China and in Burma was brutally crushed.) These experiences have contributed significantly to our understanding of the morality of non-violent resistance to oppression.

It is instructive to contrast the struggle in Peru on the one hand, and in Palestine and South Africa on the other. In Peru the liberation struggle of the 'Shining Path' movement has taken a form that is not merely violent but ruthlessly terrorist. Government forces and guerrilla forces seem to vie with each other in terrorising the local population. The result is that real liberation seems further away than ever. The leaders of the struggle for liberation of Palestine have moved in the opposite direction—away from a purely military approach. The results are remarkably successful. Two years of the 'intifada' resistance have been far more effective than thirty years of war (in varying degrees) and terrorist attacks. The Palestinians have found that for them the most effective way of resisting oppression is not an all-out military struggle. It is rather a carefully calculated and restrained opposition, combining passive resistance with mass protests and relying less on purely military means than on economic weapons such as strikes, boycotts of goods and steps towards economic self-sufficiency. An important aspect of what they have leaned is that the most effective strategy is one that does not confine active resistance to a small number of armed 'freedom fighters'. Instead it offers an opportunity to the mass of the people to be fully involved in resistance; the young people, the mothers of families and even the old people all have a part to play.

19

A study of the strategy and tactics adopted by the South African liberation movement confirms this lesson. Having had a long tradition of non-violent resistance, they felt compelled some years ago to resort to guerrilla attacks. More recently, however, the emphasis has switched back to non-violent protest actions which can involve the mass of the people.

Over the past few years, then, it has become clearer than ever before that armed insurrection is one of the least effective ways to struggle for liberation. This lesson is, in the first place, a purely pragmatic rather than a moral one. But there are important moral conclusions to be drawn; for the morality of different forms of resistance to tyranny depends to a considerable extent on the degree to which each of them is likely to be effective.

The result of all this is that people who are concerned about gross injustice in various parts of the world cannot be content with a choice between two simple options, namely, the acceptance or the rejection of armed insurrection. Instead they have to face a whole set of difficult moral questions:

—Those living inside the country have to ask themselves to what extent they ought to be actively involved in the resistance movement. Are they entitled to opt out, leaving the struggle to others? If they do become involved, what risks are they called to take, and what reservations are they entitled—or even obliged—to make? People like artists, writers, theologians, Church leaders, community leaders, trade union officials, all have to ask themselves how best they can make use of their own particular specialisation to support the liberation struggle. Among the more urgent moral issues that arise in such situations are questions about whether, or to what extent, it is permissible to use violence to resist the unjust violence of the government. This question can be answered only in the context of a careful study of whatever less violent alternatives are available—or could realistically be made available.

—People outside the country have to ask themselves what kind of support they and their countries can and ought to give to the liberation struggle. Protests? Boycotts of produce or goods? Sanctions? Guerrilla bases? Supplying arms? Supplying troops for a United Nations intervention? Armed intervention by their own country in support of the struggle? The range of options is very considerable. Before opting for the more violent courses

20

of action, individuals and governments have a serious moral obligation to work to ensure that non-violent or less violent approaches can become really effective.

5. Disarmament

I turn now to the issue of war and the threat of war *between* nations rather than *within* a particular country. I am focusing attention here, once again, on the question of the *means* that may lawfully be used to promote justice and ensure the security of people. One aspect of this question is the mediating role that can be played by international bodies such as the United Nations, the OAS (The Organization of American States), and the OAU (The Organization of African Unity). It is clear that the very existence of such bodies imposes a moral obligation on nations to make use of them for the resolution of disputes and conflicts.

When we think of war between nations the most pressing issue that springs to mind is the risk that use will be made of the really terrifying weapons that are now in the hands of many armies. In this context reflective Christians may be tempted to focus their attention mainly on working out a casuistry to spell out under what conditions it would be permissible to use various kinds of weapons, or to hold them as a deterrent—with the explicit or implicit threat that they will be used in certain circumstances. But it is far more urgent to spend our energy on finding ways to promote international disarmament—and especially the dismantling of the enormous arsenals of nuclear, bacteriological, chemical, and 'conventional' weapons possessed by the major powers.

The need for disarmament is experienced with particular vividness and urgency in Europe, situated as it is between the two super-powers. Any Europeans who stop to think, can be quite certain that they and their families have little hope of surviving a full-scale war between East and West. It is not surprising, then, that the disarmament movement is numerically strongest in Europe East and West. There is also a strong anti-nuclear movement in Oceania (particularly New Zealand) and among the peoples of the Pacific islands; for the ecological effects of the testing of atomic weapons are especially evident in that part of the world.

21

However, the newly emergent *spirituality* and theology of peace-making owes more to North America. Christian peace activists in the USA have touched the consciences of many and have influenced the thinking of Church leaders both at home and across the world. There are two main strands to this movement. One is resistance to the manufacture and holding of nuclear, bacteriological and chemical weapons as part of the policy of deterrence. The other is resistance to the US government policy of support for oppressive and dictatorial regimes in the Third World. In both of these arenas the peace activists have developed effective means of protesting against the official policy, and many have suffered harassment and imprisonment for their actions.

6. Justice for Women

I have been suggesting that the struggle against political oppression is a major item on the social justice agenda. But there is another liberation struggle going on in our world—a struggle to overcome discrimination and injustice based on gender. The issue of women's liberation is a relatively recent one. In the past there were occasions when certain aspects of this question came into prominence—mainly in the Western world; the question of voting rights for women is the most obvious instance. But there is no precedent for the extent to which 'the women's issue' has come to the top of the agenda within the past twenty years.

For many women today—and for some men—the most pressing issue of social justice is the overcoming of sexual discrimination. It is becoming ever clearer that there has been, and still is, gross discrimination on sexual grounds in every sphere of life:
—In *family* life it frequently happens that the mother is left to be responsible for almost all of the child-rearing and housekeeping, even when she is also going out to work. And because the nurturing work is largely left to women they have less opportunities to receive higher education. In poorer countries, and among the poorer classes in better-off countries, it is still quite common for the father to have much better food than the mother. There is also discrimination among the children: girls may receive less education and be expected to do a disproportionate share of the household work.
—In *public* life women are still at a great disadvantage. The kind of work that is usually done by men is generally better paid than

22

'women's work'. The medical profession (and others like it) are organised in such a way that a woman who takes time out to bear children finds it almost impossible to 'catch up' in her career prospects. Some clubs and societies still discriminate overtly against women. In business life women find it more difficult to gain promotion. In organisations of all kinds it often happens that women are expected to make the tea while the men make the decisions. In political life it is still very difficult for women to gain an equal role. In most of the major Churches and religions women are largely excluded from the top authority positions—in many cases because they are not allowed into the priesthood (or the equivalent in other religions).

—At the same time people are becoming more aware of the high degree of sexual abuse and harassment that takes place at work and in the home.

—Even the use of language has been biased against women. They are expected to see themselves as included when people use such words as 'man', 'mankind', 'brothers', etc. And in matters of religion, God is spoken of as 'he' and as a 'Lord' who calls us to a 'Kingdom'.

The issue is wider and deeper than that of overcoming overt sexual discrimination. Many feminists believe that almost all of the problems of our world today can be traced back to a typically 'male' model of exercising power. Oppression and injustice of all kinds stem from the way men have tried to dominate other people and the Earth. These feminists (men and women) are challenging in a fundamental and serious way this whole 'patriarchal' model of life, which up to the present has been the norm in most societies. They are engaging in constructing and propagating a more feminine and feminist approach to community and authority—and to the Earth itself. This new approach is more participative and collaborative, refusing to invest all authority in one leader. It is suspicious of too much rationality, stressing affectivity and intuition as a balance to purely logical or rational thought. It seeks partnership with the Earth rather than domination and exploitation.

This rejection of sexism and patriarchy arose mainly in the Western world, but is by no means confined to it. In many parts of the Third World women have become aware that they have been treated as second-class human beings; and they are now

23

rejecting this as an intolerable injustice. For a time, Third World women activists felt pulled in two opposite directions—either to work with their men towards the struggle for political and economic liberation, or to struggle against the men for liberation from male sexism. More recently they have insisted there is *one* struggle for liberation, combining these two dimensions.

7. Racism

Social injustice involves one group having an unfair advantage over others—the rich over the poor, or a repressive government over ordinary people, or men over women. Discrimination can also take place on the basis of race or ethnic origin. Then we see the particularly obnoxious form of injustice that is racism.

At times, two fairly equally balanced ethnic groups may each discriminate against the other; but more commonly there is a gross imbalance—one group has a near monopoly of power and uses it to keep the others in a subservient position. The most glaring instance of this is the crude racialism embodied in the apartheid system, which, as I write, is still the official policy of South Africa—though its days would seem to be numbered. This involves massive oppression and exploitation of the vast majority of the population, purely on the basis of racial type—or, more accurately, on the basis of an arbitrary judgment about the person's race, based on skin colour and facial features. And all this was done under the pretext of respecting the variety of ethnic groups in the country!

Racism is a set of prejudices; it involves a sense of superiority by one ethnic group over others—and a suspicion and distrust of them. Almost invariably these prejudiced attitudes are used to justify—and at the same time to cover up—a variety of unjust laws and practices. For instance, many white people in South Africa may say that the Blacks are 'irresponsible' or 'like children' and therefore cannot be allowed to vote, or that they are lazy and therefore should not be paid as much as Whites. In this way unjust political and economic structures are built upon racial or ethnic prejudice. This means that racism has become more than a set of personal attitudes: it has become solidified as part of a whole social-economic-political system.

It is easy for people in Europe or America to see such injustices in South Africa. But what about cases where economic or

24

political injustices built into our own society are expressions of *our* prejudices? Then we may be almost blind to them—for prejudice, of course, is *pre*-conscious. Blacks or immigrants or indigenous minorities in the USA or Britain are often subjected to racist treatment. And in Ireland and Britain the ethnic minority called 'Travellers' often have to put up with discrimination based on a prejudice which amounts to racism.

Somewhat similar injustices can arise even when the discrimination is not overtly based on racial grounds. Almost every country in the world has within it one or more minority groups which have their own cultures and languages. These minorities have the right to preserve their cultural identity. But, as I mentioned in the section on oppression and liberation, very commonly this right is not respected in practice. By the insensitivity of the bulk of the people, and frequently by a deliberate government policy, such minorities are pressured to conform to the ethos of the majority.

Over the centuries some groups have preserved their identity despite the pressures; one thinks of the Bretons in France, the Basques in Spain, and the Jews in many different lands. But those who live according to a traditional tribal pattern—for instance the Aboriginal people in Australia—are especially vulnerable to a combination of economic, political and cultural pressures. The discrimination to which they are subject amounts at times to a form of racism—one that puts at risk their continued existence.

8. Human Rights

Every human person is uniquely important. To be a person is to have an intrinsic value, and not merely to be important because of something extrinsic such as the work one might do. No human may be used merely as a means by somebody else. These truths are perhaps best expressed in our times by saying that each person has certain fundamental human rights. It is a matter of social justice for all of us to respect the fundamental rights of others.

The notion of human rights is so comprehensive that it can be extended to include almost the whole spectrum of social justice. So it may seem rather odd to list this topic simply as number 8 on the social justice agenda. But I am putting it down as a separate topic because to speak of respect for fundamental human rights is to adopt a distinct approach to the whole issue of social justice, one that is peculiarly modern and that is broadening and deepening all the time.

It is only in fairly recent times that the scope of human rights was extended to cover such matters as economic and cultural rights. The political philosophers who developed the notion of fundamental rights around the time of the French Revolution and the American War of Independence were thinking mainly of civil and political rights such as the right to vote or the right to a fair trial. This tradition lasted for about 150 years. The Universal Declaration of Human Rights, adopted by the United Nations in 1948 and since ratified by most countries, concentrates on political rights. This became a matter of controversy. Western politicians accused Communist nations of failing to respect the fundamental human rights of their own citizens. The response of the Easter bloc countries was to accuse the Western democracies of emphasising political rights while ignoring or playing down such fundamental economic matters as the right to work.

From the 1960s onwards the original UN charter of fundamental civil and political rights has been supplemented by further lists of social, economic and cultural rights. The lists are constantly being augmented. Quite recently, for instance, the UN adopted a set of basic rights for children. In this way the notion of human rights is extended to cover a very wide spectrum of social justice issues. Any country which succeeded in implementing all of the rights adopted at the UN would undoubtedly be a place where social justice flourishes.

One great advantage of the contemporary understanding of human rights is that it enables us to be very specific. We can say unequivocally that a regime is unjust if it does not allow its people the right to vote the government out of office, or if it does not respect the right of its citizens to freedom of conscience. But, even though many such human rights have been clearly listed, the written code of fundamental human rights cannot be used simply as a rule-book to see whether or not a particular country is practising social justice. For there are many qualifying clauses that have to be taken into account. For instance, a country will acknowledge the right of its citizens to free speech 'subject to public order' or 'subject to the needs of the common good'. Such qualifications are a practical necessity. But contro-

26

versy tends to irrupt in relation to the meaning that is given to them. Champions of human freedom often accuse governments of using the qualifications to restrict unduly the fundamental rights of the citizens.

Those who are working to build a more just world often find it helpful to articulate their struggle by saying that they are working to ensure that the various basic human rights are respected. This is both accurate and inspiring. But there is one slight weakness in expressing the struggle in this way: it could give the impression that what is involved is simply a matter of changing the laws, so that the various rights are officially recognised. The fact is, however, that a truly just world requires not merely a change in the *law* but radical changes in two other areas of life:
—firstly, change in the *attitudes* of people (especially of those who hold power) and in the traditions in which such attitudes become embodied,
—and, secondly, change in the *economic structures* of society.

The need for a change in attitudes is fairly obvious. For law can be a very inadequate instrument for bringing about justice. It is often very slow in coming into effect; and, as the saying goes, 'justice delayed is justice denied'. Even more serious is the fact that in most countries it can be very expensive to have recourse to the law. Consequently, the wealthy have a great advantage over the less well-off. This brings us to the need for a change in economic structures.

In order to bring about justice in society it is not enough to ensure that there is equality before the law. For instance, a poor person may have the *right* to take a court action against a wealthy person but may not have enough money to hire the legal experts required to win the case. Or a worker may be forced by poverty to accept an unjust wage. The same kind of thing arises at the international level in trading relations between nations. Each country may have the *right* to sell goods on the open market. But this does not ensure just trading. The poorer nations are at a great disadvantage, for they are living 'from hand to mouth', without the resources they would need to drive a hard bargain for their goods. Furthermore, they are at the mercy of the International Monetary Fund, which is controlled by the wealthy nations. International justice requires a major restructuring of the IMF.

27

It is true that when major changes eventually come about in the ownership of wealth and power they will have to be enforced by law. Nevertheless, such structural changes are not the kind of thing that immediately springs to mind when one thinks of new rights and of legal changes. For this reason, I think it is important that, when we are trying to specify the items on the social justice agenda, we do not confine ourselves exclusively to the language of human rights. Helpful though this language may be, we need to supplement it by referring also to the need for change in the economic structures of society. In fact the structural changes that are required are so extensive that they amount to the adoption of an alternative model of human development. That is a point to which I shall return later in this chapter.

9. The Population Explosion

The great increase in the population of the world, and in particular of many very poor countries is an important item on the social justice agenda. It raises urgent moral questions:

—about the responsibility of all of us to ensure that everybody has the basic necessities of a fully human life;

—about the duty of governments to strike a balance between the needs and desires of their own peoples and the pressing needs of other countries which cannot support their rapidly increasing populations;

—and about the right of governments or concerned organisations or individuals to practise or encourage or impose population control.

Concern about the rapid increase of population is not new; it goes back two centuries to the time of Malthus. But in recent years some new aspects of the question have come to the fore. One of the most important is a sharper awareness that overpopulation is an *effect* of poverty as well as its cause. Poor people in poor countries tend to have large families. This is partly because of a certain fatalism which is often linked to the belief that those who have many children are blessed by God. Furthermore, in countries where there is little or no State-supported system of social security the poor feel they need to have children so that some will survive to carry on the family and to look after the parents in their old age. Moreover, those who live a hand-to-mouth existence cannot afford to pay for sophisticated forms of birth control.

28

It is often assumed that the easiest way to ensure enough food and resources for everybody is to reduce the population (especially in Third World countries) by promoting a vigorous policy of birth control. Following this view, some governments have offered incentives to parents who limit the size of their families and have penalised those who exceed the specified limit. But if such an approach is to be effective it requires a high degree of interference by government in family life. Very many of the people affected find this unacceptable and there is widespread resistance to such policies. In practice, it is extremely difficult to control the birthrate so long as people remain very poor. Birth control campaigns on their own are not very effective in solving the problems of over-population. A much more satisfactory way of lowering the birthrate is to increase the standard of living of the people. For experience has shown that average family size falls when people are better off. So, if a government, or a voluntary organisation, or the people of the world as a whole, wish to ensure that everybody has the opportunity to live a truly human life, limitation of the birth rate can be only one element in a much larger policy of human development.

Related to this is a point which I mentioned earlier: it has now become clear that one of the major reasons for poverty in the Third World is that much of the land there is not being used to produce food for local people. Instead, it is being used to produce coffee, tea, fruit and other food goods for export to people in 'the West'. Meanwhile the local peasants go hungry for lack of land on which to grow food for themselves. This is an obvious example of unbalanced and unjust development, development that does not benefit the local population.

This leads on to the realisation that over-population has been caused largely by the application of Western technology in a one-sided way. Infant mortality has been greatly reduced by the used of modern Western medicine. But other aspects of a genuine 'human development have been grossly neglected. For instance, relatively few resources are devoted to the efficient production of food for the local people and to providing them with basic amenities such as good housing and primary health care. So what is required is a more balanced form of development which pays as much attention to the quality of adult human life as to ensuring that children do not die at a very early age.

Furthermore, it is now clear that the issue of over-population must not be posed only in terms of numbers. The number of people has to be considered in conjunction with their life-style. By and large, it is not the poor peasants of the Third World who put the greatest strain on the resources of the Earth; rather it is the affluent people—those who are living in the way that is now considered 'normal' in the wealthy nations. It has been calculated that one such person consumes more of the Earth's irreplaceable minerals and energy than fifty people living according to the traditional pattern in the so-called 'under-developed' countries. This suggests that the increase in *wasteful life-style* is perhaps more serious than the increase in the actual *numbers* of people in the world. This is not to imply that everybody ought to live at the low level endured by the poor of the Earth. But we have to find a middle way between the misery they endure and the extreme wastefulness of the affluent. Only in that context can we find a moral solution to the problems raised by the population explosion.

10. Ecology

What I have been saying about the wasteful use of resources leads on to the next major issue on the social justice agenda—the ecological question. It is a topic that has come very much to the fore in recent years. The issue concerns the whole world. But it arises in one way in the parts of the world that are technologically advanced and in a different way among people who live a more traditional life-style. In many parts of North America, Western Europe, the USSR, Japan—and in industrialised pockets of the Third World—there are serious problems about the pollution of air, land, fresh water and sea. There are also mounting worries about the way in which food is being produced and preserved. Scientists are discovering that the technology developed by other scientists poses serious threats to the health of people and to the life of the Earth itself. People are also finding that amenities they had taken for granted (pure drinking water, unpolluted seaside, etc.) may no longer be as available as they were in the past. In many places people have to live with the constant threat of an industrial or transport accident which could poison whole towns or tracts of country-side or large stretches of rivers or beaches. If such an accident should involve nuclear material the danger is almost unlimited. The Chernobyl accident gives some indication of the extent of the threat.

The ecological issue takes a somewhat different form in many Third World countries. Land is being eroded very rapidly due to over-grazing or the stripping away of the tropical forests. The desert is advancing in many semi-arid places. The cutting down of the trees means that firewood is hard to come by—and the search for fuel leads to further stripping of the land and further erosion and desertification. The resultant change in the climate forces peasants—mainly women—to walk miles carrying the water they need in their homes. The poverty of the people and of the land causes peasants to put ever greater demands on the Earth—and this in turn leads before long to greater poverty.

Quite recently these problems have been greatly increased by the fact that the more industrialised countries have been trying to lessen their own ecological problems by exporting some of them to the Third World. Toxic industrial waste, and even radioactive materials, have been dumped in poorer countries by unscrupulous companies. Governments in these countries may not have available to them the technological expertise to monitor the waste material; or officials may be bribed to allow dangerous dumping to take place.

Besides this, multinational companies have established dangerous and polluting industries in Third World countries where safety and monitoring standards are less stringent. So there is the risk of further dreadful accidents like that which took place in a chemical factory at Bhopal in India, in which thousands were killed or seriously injured. Even more risky is the development of nuclear energy in some Third World countries. First World scientists and governments often express alarm about this proliferation. There may well be an element of colonialism or even racism in such alarm. But the fact is that the use of nuclear power is inherently dangerous; and the more widely it is used the greater the danger. And in some of the newly developing countries the controls on the way it is used may be even less stringent than in Western countries.

Some of the ecological abuses of the Third World are affecting the world as a whole. The most obvious example is the wholesale cutting down of the tropical rain-forests in Brazil, Africa, Indonesia, etc. Many reputable scientists believe that the loss of

31

oxygen produced by these forests, and the smoke from their burning, are bringing about a 'greenhouse effect' which will raise the average temperature all over the world. This, they say, will in turn lead to the melting of huge amounts of ice at the North and South Poles. The resultant rise in the water level of the oceans may cause much of Bangladesh and other heavily-populated low-lying areas to be totally engulfed by the sea.

So far I have dealt with the ecological question purely in terms of its effects on humans. But more and more people are coming to believe that there are wider issues at stake. Animals and plants share this Earth with us. Do we have an unlimited right to use them and abuse them solely for our own convenience? Does it make sense to speak of animal rights? Should we accept that even the Earth itself has a right to flourish? Religious believers may pose these questions in a different way: when we humans were given a share in God's creative power were we given unconditional dominion over the Earth? Or do we have obligations to care for the Earth and its species, even if this imposes limits on the kind of development we may promote?

11. Refugees

Serious famines or food shortages in several countries of the Third World have arisen as a result of crop failures brought about by drought, pests, or natural disasters of various kinds. But why are poorer countries so much more liable to such catastrophes? Mainly for two reasons:

—firstly because, being poor, they live 'nearer to the edge'—i.e. they cannot afford to build up the stocks of food and money that would tide them over difficult periods;

—secondly, because in many cases they suffer from over-population in relation to the resources available to them and the accessibility of technology that would enable them to use their resources more effectively. As I pointed out in the previous two sections, over-population leads to over-grazing, erosion, the cutting down of forests and the advance of the deserts. This in turn leads to even greater poverty.

Sudden or chronic famine may become so severe that large numbers of people may have no other option than to leave their homes in search of food. Such *economic* refugees are one aspect of the refugee problem.

There are also *political* refugees—people forced to flee their homes because of cruel wars in which modern military tactics and weapons make life a nightmare for the civilian population. In many cases famine and the creation of economic refugees is used deliberately as a weapon of war. At the time of writing this seems to be the case in southern Sudan; it is also the policy of the Mozambique rebels who are supported by South Africa with the aim of destabilising a neighbouring country which might be hostile to it.

Then there is the more traditional kind of political refugee. Many of them come from segments of the population of certain countries that are persecuted on racial/ethnic grounds or on the basis of their religious beliefs or political views. In other cases a change of regime has left formerly privileged groups with a strong feeling of insecurity or harassment—to a point where some of them leave their homes and seek asylum in other countries.

The combination of some or all of these problems has given rise to an enormous increase in the numbers of refugees. A small minority of highly skilled refugees may be welcomed in other countries because of their skills. But the real refugee problem arises when there are very large numbers of impoverished people fleeing from famine, war, persecution or insecurity, to countries that do not want them and cannot afford to keep them. Major moral issues arise in this situation.

In the short term, two important moral questions have to be answered:

—Whose responsibility is it to look after the immediate basic needs of refugees who come streaming over the borders of a poor country into a country that may be equally impoverished?

—How can this be done in a way that leaves the refugees their dignity and self-respect, and that does not infringe their cultural rights; and how can refugees be given the help they need without alienating the sympathy of the people among whom they have come to live, and who may soon see strangers getting help that is not available to the local people?

Long-term moral issues also arise:

—To what extent are the people of distant wealthy nations obliged to take responsibility for refugees by allowing them to come and settle among them?

—If refugees are allowed to come, how is their distinct cultural heritage to be protected?

33

12. Unemployment

The use of modern technology has been the key factor in recent Western-style development. More and more sophisticated machines have made it possible for ordinary people to obtain the necessities of life—and many luxuries as well—without being chained for endless hours to the drudgery of heavy manual labour. But when more efficient machinery is installed the same amount of products can be made by a smaller number of workers. Consequently, the higher the technology the less employment is available—unless new markets can be found for the extra goods, or the redundant workers find new jobs in providing different goods and services.

In the past there was generally more work to be done than could be accomplished by the available work-force. But at the present time mass production, automation and computerisation have brought about a major shift in the balance between the work that is available and the workers available to do it. If all available industrial workers were fully employed in industry they would produce far more goods than could be sold or used. And automation is causing this gap between supply and demand to grow ever wider. Obviously, the gap has to be narrowed and there are only three ways to do it:

(1) The demand can be greatly stimulated by advertising and by lowering the price of the items to be sold.

(2) The supply can be scaled down by a refusal to use the higher forms of automation.

(3) Alternatively, the supply can be reduced to the size of the demand by putting more and more people out of work.

It used to be assumed that there was room for more or less unlimited expansion in the demand for goods and services—provided the demand was stimulated by lowering the cost and by advertising. In fact the presupposition of the Western economic system was that the secret of success was continual growth in demand. But now we have to take account of both ecological and practical/economic limits to growth:

—From an ecological point of view, unlimited growth is unacceptable and even impossible; the Earth does not have the resources for such growth. Therefore, what we have to learn is how to make judicious choices about where to allow growth and where to cut back.

—From a practical/economic point of view, the failure of Western-style development plans in many Third World countries and the burden of debt which weighs them down have severely limited the extent to which the West can use these countries as markets for its products.

The conclusion that emerges clearly is that there is no likelihood that sufficient new jobs can be found for workers displaced by the use of ever higher technology. Unemployment is no longer a temporary by-product of our economic system—an interval while workers move from one job to another. The fact that a high percentage of workers have no job cannot even be seen as the result of a fairly short-term breakdown of the economic system such as occurred for several years during the Great Depression of the 1930s. Large-scale unemployment has become chronic and apparently irreversible. That is why economists and others now speak of 'structural unemployment'; the phrase indicates that large-scale unemployment is virtually an intrinsic part of the present-day economic structures of society. No wonder then that in many Western countries this chronic inability of most modern economies to create new jobs for the unemployed has become one of the most urgent social issues of all.

The best that many governments can do is to provide retraining schemes. Such schemes were first designed for situations where those who become unemployed in one sector of the economy can be redeployed into another sector which is in need of employees; and under these conditions they can be fairly successful. But at present they have only a very limited success since the overall number of available jobs is far less than the number of the unemployed. Indeed such retraining schemes may be seen as a way in which governments disguise their failure to face up to the real problem of unemployment.

In the so-called developed countries, workers who fail to get a job usually get an unemployment 'handout' from the State to enable them to survive. But it is becoming more and more evident that even generous social welfare benefits are no solution to the problem of structural unemployment. Respectability in modern society is closely related to 'having a job'; therefore the jobless person feels a failure and a misfit. Perhaps the social stigma of being unemployed could be lessened by a major programme of re-education. But education alone cannot solve the problem. For those who have no job are bound to remain at or very near the bottom of society and this affects how they are seen by themselves and others. More fundamentally, all human beings know deep down that they are workers by nature. Consequently, it is highly likely that people who have lost their job will become demoralised and alienated—unless they are able to find other rewarding work.

The problem of structural unemployment also affects the many Third World countries that adopted the Western model of development, pinning their hopes on industrialisation and the mechanisation of agriculture. In these countries the problems of large-scale chronic unemployment are even greater: trade unions are often ineffective, so workers are left unprotected; and social security systems are minimal. However, the unemployed in the Third World often have far more initiative than those who have no jobs in the wealthy countries; this is because they have not come to depend so totally on the State to solve their problems. Furthermore, they are more likely to have the possibility of going back to the land to eke out a living there.

13. Alternative Model of Development

Within the present main economic and political structures of the world it might be possible to find solutions to some of the problems I have listed on previous pages. But two items stand out as quite intractable so long as the present model of economics holds sway. The first is the ecological issue and the second is structural unemployment. The problems under these two headings arise as a result of the basic drive that lies at the heart of modern Western economics and 'development'—the drive to produce and sell more and more goods as *cheaply* and *efficiently* as possible.

The core of the difficulty lies in the way the two words 'cheap' and 'efficient' are understood. At present, most manufacturers have convincing reasons for changing over to automated machinery even if that involves making many employees redundant. But that is only because they as manufacturers do not have to pay the full human and social costs of unemployment. So the current criteria for calculating cheapness and efficiency are inadequate and inaccurate; they do not include the hidden and long-term costs. Other examples: the owner of a badly insulated house may find it less expensive to pay the extra costs of heating rather than pay for effective insulation; but this is because the current cost of oil and gas does not take account of the ecological cost of wasted energy. Again, it is cheaper to produce beef by adding growth-promoting steroids to the foodstuff of the cattle; but this does not take sufficient account of the health risks to those who eat the meat. In each of these cases there are long-term costs which are not paid by the person who controls the product and makes decisions on the basis of short-term gains. If *all* the costs were taken into account it would often be more efficient and less costly to take a different course of action than the one that seems cheapest and most efficient according to present criteria.

Efficiency remains an important economic and human value. But it has to be defined in a way that takes account of *all* the costs that are involved; and this will lead to the exclusion of many shortcuts that have been taken in the past. Such a redefinition is no minor matter. It involves a very radical reappraisal of the fundamental elements of the Western economic system. To implement it would amount to the adoption of a very different model of human development. It is not easy to specify in detail what this would look like. Some committed individuals, families and communities have succeeded in working out alternatives on a small scale. But these can only be seen as partial experiments, for the real test is whether they can be implemented on a large scale—eventually, on a world scale.

It is clear that a morally acceptable model of human development should incorporate certain basic values:
—It would need to be sustainable from an ecological point of view, so that it respects the rights of future generations to a fair share of the resources of the Earth. This means that it would have to embody genuine respect for the Earth itself and be based on partnership with nature rather than exploitation.
—It should be an approach that makes fulfilling work available to all who wish to work; this means that nobody should be condemned to drudgery or to the alienation that arises when workers are unable to have a personal involvement in the product that is produced or a say in determining the conditions of their work. Above all, it means that people should not be forced into a situation where, over a long period, they are effectively denied the opportunity of doing real work.

—It should be an approach that avoids the mistake of identi-fying 'work' with 'employment'. It seems likely that any successful future model of human development will involve having less people who are working as employees for others; instead there will be many more workers' cooperatives as well as more self-employed people.

—It would have to provide incentives to promote efficiency; but equally there should be incentives to encourage quality, safety, and ecological responsibility. There is also need for incentives to encourage workers to play an active part in planning their work, and to develop a friendly and supportive environment in the work-place.

—In addition, the alternative model of development should be one that enables ordinary people to be far more involved than at present in making the decisions that affect their lives; in other words, the appropriate style of development is one that is com-patible with, and even promotes, participative decision-making in *all* spheres of life, and not merely in the places where people work.

Of course all this sounds like a utopian dream. Even the most optimistic planner must admit that it would take many years to implement such values fully. And any realist can see that in practice it is highly unlikely that such an alternative model of development will ever be adopted on a large scale. But our present economic system is so grossly unjust that it cannot be defended from a moral point of view. And it is so inadequate from a human and ecological point of view that it is running into very grave problems. So we need to develop some ideal of a more moral and effective model of development. The ideal could help those who believe that the present system can be reformed from within in a piecemeal and gradual way. It may also inspire those who are trying to opt out of the present system and seeking to build an alternative 'from the ground up'. In a later chapter of this book I shall consider whether Christians have any particular contribution to make to the search for an alternative model of development, which is perhaps the most comprehensive and fundamental issue of the whole social justice agenda. But I want first to finish this chapter by giving some account of what I see as the final item on the social justice agenda, namely, justice within the Church itself.

14. Justice in the Church

Christians have to give a high place on the social justice agenda to justice within the Church. The primary way in which the Church teaches about justice is not by proclaiming a list of principles. Rather it is by its lived witness to its beliefs, its values, and its opinions. The Church's proclaimed principles should be echoed in the attitudes of the Christian community and its leaders—both in relation to the Church's own members and in relation to others. If there were a flagrant disparity between the official teaching and the way the Church lives, acts, and organises itself, then the teaching would be lacking in credibility. It would even be incoherent, contradictory, and meaningless. The words without the witness are not truth. The Epistle of St James suggests that to rely on the spoken word alone is to look in the mirror but then forget what one saw (1:22-4); it is not merely useless but even demonic, for it means having the same kind of faith as the demons (2:14-24).

Until fairly recent times there was a certain consistency between the proclaimed social teaching of most of the mainline Churches and their actual practice. Two examples of this:

(1) Early in this century the social teaching in several Churches placed a rather one-sided emphasis on the right to private property; and this proclaimed truth was matched by a hostility, in practice, to socialism.

(2) From the sixteenth century up to about the sixties of this century, the teaching of many Church leaders laid great stress on the God-given authority of kings and queens and of the State. This was matched in practice by a rather escapist spirituality which encouraged oppressed people to look for reward in the next life while here on earth they should submit to injustice and endure repression rather than struggling for liberation.

Within the past generation there has been a major change in emphasis in official Church teaching on such matters, and in the whole understanding of justice. This has given rise to the problem of the rather wide gap which has opened up between the new proclaimed teaching and the actual structures and policies of the Church. To the extent that such a gap persists, it makes the Church's teaching on justice and peace incoherent—and even a counter-witness to truth. The gap between theory and practice has opened up precisely because the Churches really listened to

39

prophetic voices and through them allowed the Spirit to challenge the Church. So we can be rather proud of the gap— provided we are trying to bridge it! This means acknowledging that in many ways the Church itself stands under the judgment of its own teaching. And it means undertaking the painful task of correcting our inadequacies and failures.

This is a moment of truth for Church leaders and for individual Christians. Church teaching on social justice has been worked out fairly comprehensively. What remains is the challenge of trying to live by it. Church leaders may be tempted to substitute rhetoric for action, turning the Church into a mere verbal champion of justice and peace. Strong affirmations of human rights are good; and so too are ringing condemnations of oppression. But far more important is whether the Church gives practical support 'on the ground' to oppressed people struggling for their human rights, instead of holding itself at a certain distance from them.

Another great temptation for Christians—and, especially for Church leaders—is to play down the issue of justice within the Church itself. To do so would damage the Church's credibility. I can illustrate the challenge by referring to the situation in the Roman Catholic Church which, being my home, is the Church I know best. The 1971 Synod of Bishops in Rome represents a high point in the Catholic Church's attempt to bridge the gap between theory and practice. The Synod document, 'Justice in the World', contains the following striking passage:

> While the Church is bound to give witness to justice it recognizes that anyone who ventures to speak to people about justice must first be just in their eyes. Therefore, we must undertake an examination of the modes of acting and of the possessions and life-style within the Church itself. (No. 40)

The Synod document insisted on the right of participation— the right of ordinary members of the Church to be involved in its decision-making processes (No. 46). In recent years the Vatican has taken some important steps towards an implementation of this principle. In the new Code of Canon Law there is a strong insistence on the importance of advisory councils at diocesan and parish level—pastoral councils, finance councils, etc. In some areas these new structures are operating quite effectively. In other areas, unfortunately, the clergy have been very reluctant to let go of 'their' power.

In its treatment of justice in the Church the Synod document went much further than calling for advisory councils. It noted the need to look again at the way in which certain categories of people are treated in the Church: lay employees, the laity as a whole, women in general, women religious, people involved in judical procedures (Nos. 41-5).

The Synod Fathers were not content with exhortations. They made a very practical proposal: that a serious study of justice in the Church be made by 'a mixed commission of men and women, religious and lay people, of differing situations and competence' (No. 43). That proposal was made by the Synod nearly twenty years ago but it has not yet been acted upon. Furthermore, around the time of the 1971 Synod the idea of having a charter of fundamental rights in the Church was in the air; but there is no indication that Rome is willing to take up this proposal.

The fourteen issues which I have outlined in this chapter form the bulk of what I am calling 'the social justice agenda'. Some of the issues are as old as human society; others have emerged for the first time, or have come into prominence, only in recent years. Church teaching on questions related to justice and peace has evolved over the years as an attempt to provide some guidance for Christians in relation to these issues. In the following chapters I shall examine the development of Christian social teaching and I shall indicate what the Churches have to say at present about the major issues of justice and peace.

PART TWO
The Teaching of the Churches

2

The Development of Catholic Social Teaching

WHEN WE LOOK back on the spirituality which moulded the attitudes of many of the present generation of Church leaders and committed Christians during their 'formative years' we can see that it was very inadequate in its social dimensions. This narrow spirituality was picked up either through formal courses or as part of the general atmosphere of the time. It left many of us with the notion that our relationship with God is first and foremost a personal/private affair. We now realise that spirituality must have a very strong social dimension. So we feel called to make a major shift in our attitudes. Such a shift can be both confusing and disturbing. However, the confusion can be lessened by bringing out clearly the elements of continuity and discontinuity between the present agenda and the older one. And the sense of disturbance can be allayed if we come to understand what lay behind the older spirituality and to see why the Churches expanded their horizons on social issues. So a study of the historical background to the present social justice agenda can strengthen and support us in developing a more balanced spirituality.

At the present time most of the main Christian Churches have social justice agendas that are very similar to each other; in fact their approach is almost identical on most socio-political questions. (Later on I shall say something about some fundamentalist-evangelical Churches or sects that adopt a very different approach.) In the past, however, there were very notable differences between the mainline Churches—and they travelled along quite different paths. It was only in relatively recent times that they realised that their paths were converging. In this chapter I shall give a brief account of the development of the social justice teaching of the Catholic Church. In the next chapter I shall go on to examine the parallel development in the World Council of Churches. I believe that an understanding of the journey travelled by the Churches in this century may be of help to people who are in the process of making a similar journey for themselves.

The Catholic Church has, of course, always seen itself as having a teaching role on social issues. But it is especially in the past hundred years, with the issuing of a series of social encyclicals, that the concept of a coherent body of 'social teaching' has emerged. This is official teaching, promulgated mainly by the highest authority in the Catholic Church. So it is not just the views of theologians—though of course the theologians contributed greatly to the formation of the teaching.

I shall begin this account by giving a brief indication of some of the main concerns of the authorities of the Catholic Church in the period prior to 1960. Then I shall look at the changes of direction or emphasis that began with Pope John XXIII in 1961 and were strongly affirmed in Vatican II. Next I shall indicate the importance of the Medellín Conference of 1968, which contributed so much to the present social justice agenda. Finally, I shall note some of the more recent developments in Catholic teaching.

Prior to Pope John
It is important to recognise that the teaching and attitudes of Church leaders on social issues were not worked out by a systematic deductive process. Rather they developed in an *ad hoc* way in reaction to particular sets of historical circumstances. This older agenda took shape over about a hundred years between 1860 and 1960. Many factors contributed to it but here I shall mention just three particularly formative influences.[1]

Firstly, there was the plight of millions of industrial workers, people who were employed in the factories and mines that had sprung up in the newly industrialised parts of Europe and North America. The hours of work were very long, working conditions were frequently appalling, child labour was often used, and social services were minimal. It was this situation that led Pope Leo XIII to issue the first of the great social encyclicals, *Rerum Novarum* in 1891. (The title may be translated as 'The Modern Situation'.)

46

Secondly, a number of European countries had gone through the experience of revolution or attempted revolution; in some cases this had led to very severe disruption of society. Church authorities reacted very strongly against the revolutionary movements. They insisted that the authority of civil governments came from God. Leo XIII concluded that protests against unjust actions by governments are legitimate only when they are non-violent. Pius XI, however, suggested that it might be lawful to go further in certain very special circumstances.

Thirdly, Church authorities and theologians developed their social teaching in reaction to what they saw as the errors and aberrations of many Western political philosophers. These Church leaders were particularly concerned about two very different trends, which may be roughly described as left-wing and right-wing.

The left-wing 'errors' covered everything from extreme anarchism to mild versions of socialism, or even what would now be called social democracy. These were frequently 'lumped together' and all 'tarred with the same brush'.

The right-wing philosophy that Church leaders rejected all through this period was economic liberalism and the political individualism that was linked to it; these provided the ideological basis for capitalism. In the Church's eyes the crucial error in this thinking was a playing down of the organic unity of society, and a consequent misunderstanding of the nature of human authority. In the 1930s the Church had to make a stand against a different version of right-wing philosophy—National Socialism (the Nazi philosophy) and related forms of fascist thinking. As the Church saw it, these philosophies were tainted with the same fundamental error as communism and socialism, namely, the total subordination of the individual to the State or the collectivity. This meant that both left-wing and right-wing regimes could be guilty of State absolutism.

During the early part of the twentieth century Catholic Church authorities still had a rather ambivalent attitude to democracy. Insisting that God is the source of all authority, they rejected the notion that political power came 'from below' (from the people). As more and more States adopted democratic structures, Catholic Church leaders rather grudgingly acknowledged that democracy could be a legitimate form of government. However, over the years—and especially after World War II— the Church came to see democracy in a much more favourable light.

What emerges from all this is that during the early part of this century the Church had a fairly coherent body of social teaching. It had developed at a time when the Catholic Church was a conservative force in society and was resistant to the new philosophical and theological ideas that had emerged in recent centuries. This social doctrine provided the theoretical underpinning for the practical political stance taken by Church leaders and the Church as an institution. That stance was an odd mixture of apparently disparate ingredients. On the one hand there was a strong streak of social conservatism. But on the other hand there were elements of a radical critique of the prevailing Western model of capitalism—springing from a very real concern for the poor.

Not all aspects of this body of social teaching were equally absolute. Some were concerned with fundamental values; while others had to do only with the means that seemed appropriate at a particular time for the attainment of these values.

A Catholic Blueprint for Society

There was a major crisis of capitalism in the years following the Wall Street crash on the New York stock exchange in 1929. It was a time of great suffering and bitterness for very large numbers of workers who suddenly found themselves out of work, with little or no social security. Tensions between the classes sharpened and many workers and intellectuals became convinced that the way forward was a complete replacement of capitalism by a communist or socialist system. At the same time there was a great upsurge of right-wing movements which proposed a fascist solution to social problems. The fascists' approach involved an odd mixture of capitalistic and socialistic elements. They retained the concept of private enterprise but they wanted the State to play a much more active role in economic affairs than in traditional capitalistic society.

A central aspect of the fascist approach to economics and politics was a design for society that would eliminate or minimise the possibility of class struggle. The aim was to ensure that the traditional division of society into upper and lower classes would be overcome by dividing society instead into various vocational groupings or 'corporations' (e.g. the agricultural

48

sector, the business sector, etc). Within each of the different corporations or vocational groupings there would be people of different social classes. As a result, people would no longer be motivated by the interests of the *class* to which they belonged; instead, their interests would be tied to that of their particular vocational grouping in its dialogue with other such groupings. This was the system adopted by the fascists in Italy and other right-wing regimes in Europe.

Pope Pius XI had serious reservations about the overall philosophy of fascism and he was concerned about their style of politics. Nevertheless, he was impressed by some of the achievements of the fascists in Italy. He was also disposed to look somewhat more favourably on them because of the successful outcome of negotiations between the Vatican and the Italian State in the Lateran treaty. Looking at the apparently effective new model of society adopted by the fascists, the pope thought it might provide an alternative to both socialism and the more common form of capitalism. The Church had always been very strongly opposed to the Marxist notion of class war. At the same time Pius XI could see that the capitalist system had brought about major injustice in society—and, furthermore, it no longer seemed to be working successfully even according to its own values. So, in his 1931 social encyclical *Quadragesimo Anno* he recommended the corporatist or vocational system in rather vague general terms.

The idea of the vocational organisation of society was taken up enthusiastically by many Catholic social activists. All during the 1930s and well into the 1940s it became a key element in Catholic social teaching. Catholic leaders and theologians presented it as *the* blueprint for a socially just society.

After World War II this whole approach began to be seen as quite unrealistic (partly because it seemed to some to be tinted with discredited fascist philosophy). Pope Pius XII still paid a kind of notional allegiance to the idea. But it was clear that for him it had a rather low priority. Far more urgent in his mind was the belief that 'the West' had to strengthen itself against the threat of communism; in practice, this meant an acceptance of a somewhat softened version of capitalism. Nevertheless, up to the time of Pope John XXIII the notion of the vocational organisation of society remained part of Catholic social teaching—at least as a kind of vague ideal. Since about 1960 the idea has been quietly dropped.

49

A Change of Direction: Pope John's Contribution

During the 1960s the Church made a serious effort to catch up with new thinking and to re-examine its role in the world. This left it in a better position to face up to the major changes that have been taking place in society over the past generation. The effect of all this on the social teaching of the Church was quite considerable. While retaining a significant degree of continuity with the past, the teaching changed notably in emphasis and direction.

Changes in the Catholic Church are often dated from the Second Vatican Council. But as regards social teaching, the first major step in a new direction was taken in 1961, the year *before* the Council, when Pope John XXIII issued the encyclical *Mater et Magistra*, the first social encyclical for thirty years. In doing this, Pope John was making a definite option: he was deliberately setting out to change the thrust and the effect of the Church's social teaching.

One reason why Pope John wanted changes was that his own peasant background made him more sympathetic than earlier popes to the views of working-class people. A more profound reason was his openness to the Spirit and his understanding of the Gospel. This enabled him to realise that something had gone wrong with Catholic social teaching. He saw that secondary elements in it had come to take priority over primary elements. Concern for the rights of property owners had taken precedence over concern for the poor; and concern for stability had taken precedence over concern for justice.

The result of this distortion was that the social teaching of the Church—particularly its emphasis on the right to private property—was being used ideologically. To illustrate this point we can note that in Italy the traditional Church condemnation of socialism was being invoked by some senior Vatican cardinals as a basis for aligning themselves with right-wing forces and opposing the 'opening to the left' (*apertura a sinistra*) which was taking place after 1960 both in Italian politics and at the international level.

Pope John wanted to distance the Church from such entanglements with right-wing political forces. He also wanted to distance it again (as had been done by Leo XIII and Pius XI) from the ideology of economic liberalism which provides the theoretical underpinning for crude capitalism. He wanted to ensure that Church teaching could not be invoked either in support of economic liberalism or in favour of right-wing politics.

He was well aware that he had a big struggle on his hands. And he was at a disadvantage; for he could not even rely on the cooperation of the heads of the Vatican curia.[2] The seventieth anniversary of the publication of Leo's *Rerum Novarum* offered him an ideal opportunity to issue his new social encyclical. *Mater et Magistra* ('Mother and Teacher'). In it he reaffirmed the basic thrust of Catholic social teaching. But he also set out 'to determine clearly the mind of the Church on the new and important problems of the day' (par. 50). It was in this context that he introduced a shift of direction and of emphasis in social teaching.

What was the new emphasis? One element was that John came out in favour of something that sounded rather like the Welfare State. A second element was his strong affirmation that the right to own private property is subordinate to a more fundamental principle, namely, that the goods of the earth are intended for the use and benefit of all. Although this had been accepted in medieval times, Leo XIII had played it down because of his fear of socialism. Pius XII, in his 1941 broadcast commemorating the fiftieth anniversary of *Rerum Novarum*, had spelled it out clearly. But, coming in the middle of World War II, this had made little impact. The idea was now given considerable prominence by John XXIII. The effect was that the right to private property became a matter of relative importance rather than a fundamental principle, as it had effectively become in Catholic social teaching over the previous century.

One result of this change of emphasis was an outraged reaction by right-wing Catholics. Their attitude was summed up in the phrase: '*Mater si, Magistra no*' ('Mother yes, teacher no'). It was their reaction, perhaps more than the content of the new encyclical, that brought about the most significant change of all. This was a change not so much in the actual teaching as in the public perception of the stance of the official Church. For the first time in at least a hundred years the Church seemed to lean more towards the left than towards the right. It was at this moment that the Church began to have new allies and new enemies.

51

The Contribution of Vatican II

Where does Vatican II come in this change of emphasis and direction? If the Council had not taken place it is quite likely that Pope John's new emphasis would not have lasted; it would have been watered down by Vatican officials and/or by a later pope. But the climate created by Vatican II made it almost impossible for any pope to reverse John's new direction. Almost as soon as the Council opened in 1962 it rejected the reactionary views of those who opposed him. Three years later it issued its own teaching on issues of justice and peace in the document entitled *Gaudium et Spes* ('The Church in the Modern World'). The Council followed Pope John's new line. In fact it went further than him by insisting that the goods of the earth are destined by God not only for all *people* but also for all *peoples* (GS 69.1), thus opening up the whole major issue of a just international economic order, and providing a solid theological basis for the Council's own teaching on this subject (GS 85). This in turn was followed up in Pope Paul's encyclical *Populorum Progressio* ('On the Development of Peoples'), issued in 1967, which spelled out in considerable detail the Church's new understanding of international social justice.

The Council also added some other important elements to the new synthesis of social teaching which was emerging at this time.[3] Here I shall simply note four points:

1. *Gaudium et Spes* ('The Church in the Modern World') firmly linked the political issue of peace between nations to the issue of a just international economic order (GS 83-7). When Pope Paul set up the Vatican Justice and Peace Office he was following this Council line. The link between justice and peace is now so taken for granted that the phrase 'justice and peace' trips off the tongues of Church people like an old cliché; and we may forget that it is relatively recent.

2. Vatican II proposed a concept of human development which underpins the present body of Catholic social teaching (GS 63-6). This was a major contribution of the Council to the theology of the world. I must add that in recent years the Council's teaching on development has had to be modified considerably, particularly by toning down its unwarranted optimism.

3. The Council insisted that it is not merely the superfluous goods, the left-overs, of the rich which are to be given to the

52

poor (GS 69.1); rather, the poor have a right to a fair share of the earth's resources. Applying this principle in practice the Council envisaged the expropriation of under-utilised large estates (GS 76.6).

4. Finally, the Council affirmed that the Church is willing to relinquish the exercise of legitimately acquired rights in situations where holding on to them would compromise its witness (GS 76). This is one of the most important acts of Vatican II, for (as we shall see) it opened the way to a relinquishment by the Church of the political privileges which it had enjoyed in traditionally Catholic countries, such as Spain and Italy and, above all, the Latin American countries.

We may note in passing that there are some gaps in the teaching of the Council. One of the most notable of these was deliberate: there is no treatment of the question of the lawfulness of wars of liberation. An early draft of the document *The Church in the Modern World* included a passage which recognised a parallel between a just war and justified resistance to oppression (i.e. rebellion). When this met with some criticism it was simply deleted. The Council Fathers and theologians decided that they did not have time to work out a consensus statement on this sensitive issue. They chose to give their time and energy to working out a strong statement on the topic of war *between* States rather than on liberation struggles *within* States.

From what I have said it should be clear that, while Vatican II did not say the final word on the present social justice agenda, it did have a major influence on it. The contribution of the Council may be summed up under three headings:

—Firstly, as regards what had gone before it: the Council supported unequivocally Pope John's distancing of the Church from the right wing.

—Secondly, Vatican II made its own distinctive contribution; this consisted mainly in providing a theology of human development, an enriched theology of peace, and a firm link between the two.

—Thirdly, Vatican II provided the foundation for a radically new approach in the future, a future that was not explicitly envisaged by the Council Fathers themselves, but which nevertheless sprang directly from the Council. I want now to develop this point more fully.

At the conference in Medellín in 1968 the Church leaders of Latin America set out to implement and apply the Vatican Council in their own situation. This conference made a decisive contribution to the new justice and peace agenda—not merely for Latin America but for the whole Church. No significant statement about justice made after 1968 could fail to take account of the Medellín documents. They introduced a new approach, a new language, and a new option:

—A new approach: they began from an analysis of the concrete situation rather than repeating traditional doctrine.

—A new language: they provided the Church with a whole new set of terms and concepts which nowadays we can scarcely imagine being without, e.g. 'structural injustice', 'institutionalised violence', 'marginalisation', 'liberation', 'conscientisation', and 'participation';

—A new option: having carefully clarified the different senses of the word 'poverty', the bishops deliberately committed themselves to:

(a) being in solidarity with the poor;

(b) giving an effective 'preference to the poorest and most needy sectors' of society;

(c) seeking true peace not by promoting stability but by arousing the consciousness of oppressed groups and helping them organise to become agents of their own development.

The approach, the language, and the option of Medellín became, in the years that followed, a sign of contradiction both in the Latin American Church itself and almost everywhere else in the world, including Rome. In order to understand the real meaning of various subsequent papal documents and statements one has to understand them as at least partly a response to what was said at Medillín. So a very large part of the present justice and peace agenda springs from Medellín rather than directly from Vatican II.

However, there can be no serious doubt that, without the Council, the Medellín Conference would have had a very different outcome. There are three main ways in which the Council gave rise to Medellín:

54

(i) It ratified the option of Pope John to disengage the Church from right-wing and ultra-conservative regimes.

(ii) *Gaudium et Spes* put forward a new model of Church-State relationships, one that specifically envisaged the relinquishment by the Church of privileges granted by the State.

(iii) It opened up the Latin American bishops to the notion that the Spirit might be calling them to a radical change of approach; so they were able to hear the prophetic voices of people like Helder Camara and emerging theologians such as Gustavo Gutiérrez.

One can conclude that Vatican II made Medellín possible, even though much of the approach, the language, and the commitment of Medellín are a major advance on the Council.

In taking this new approach and new option, and in using the new language, the bishops at Medellín were accepting as their own the liberation theology that was just emerging at that time in Latin America. The remarkable thing was that this radically new theology was almost immediately adopted at the official level of the Conference of Latin American bishops. In fact it is not an exaggeration to say that the Medellín documents were themselves among the early articulations of liberation theology.

Implicit in the new theology was a new spirituality. At first, this found expression more in action and in liturgical celebrations than in books. But in recent years the spirituality of liberation has been articulated in depth in various books and articles.[4] In fact it is difficult to draw a sharp line of distinction between the theology and the spirituality of liberation. This in itself is a major contribution to the renewal both of theology and of spirituality.

What is significant about liberation spirituality/theology— and about the Medellín documents which are themselves liberationist in tone and content—is not simply that they represent a positive response by the Church to suffering, poverty, and injustice. More important is the fact that they represent a positive response by the Church to the *struggle to overcome oppression* and unjust poverty. Church leaders who adopt a liberationist stance acknowledge that it may not be sufficient merely to call on the rich and powerful to stop oppressing the poor; so they are willing to offer encouragement and practical support to those who organise themselves to overcome oppression. Their most important contribution to the struggle for liberation is the fact that

55

they offer religious justification to those who take the risk of challenging injustice. This does not mean that these Church leaders have begun to promote revolution. But they no longer present stability as the overriding political value.

It would be difficult to overemphasise the influence that the new agenda of the Latin American Church has had on certain key sectors of the Catholic Church. Its influence has been felt above all in religious orders and congregations and in missionary societies. Almost without exception these have been engaged over the past fifteen years in a very radical re-think of their role in society and the Church. Clear evidence for this can be found in the extent to which they have incorporated 'solidarity with the poor' or 'option for the poor' or similar phrases into their 'vision statements' or 'mission statements', or even into the revised text of their Constitutions. The members of the different congregations are gradually drawing out the practical implications of these statements and they have begun to implement them. This is bringing about a most significant change of direction—one of the biggest changes that has ever occurred in religious life. One result has been the emergence of a widening gap between the thinking and practice of the religious congregations on the one hand and the Vatican and most diocesan clergy on the other.

Other sectors of the Catholic Church have also been greatly affected by this new agenda; the extent of its influence varies greatly from place to place. In Zimbabwe, South Africa, The Philippines, Korea and many other countries, bishops have taken a very strong stance for justice and liberation. In most countries there is now a considerable degree of polarisation. On the one hand, certain groups of laity, priests, and some religious congregations have adopted a strongly 'liberationist' stance. Meanwhile others are extremely critical of liberation theology and spirituality.

The Pontificate of Paul VI

The greatest achievement of Paul VI was to steer Vatican II to a successful conclusion and to oversee the practical implementation of the direction it set and the guidelines it laid down. In the years after the Council, four documents of major significance for the social justice agenda were issued by Rome.[5] The first of these was the pope's social encyclical *Populorum Progressio* ('On the

Development of Peoples') which was issued in 1967. In it he proposed a carefully thought out theology of development—and not merely economic development but also taking account of social, political, and cultural aspects. He also took a stand against the kind of economic domination of poorer countries which is called 'neo-colonialism' (though he does not use this term); and he called for a new international economic order. In a brief and very cautiously worded statement—which is nevertheless extremely important—he acknowledged that in certain extreme circumstances a revolutionary uprising might be permissible (No. 31); this statement was used (and taken a small step further) in the following year by the Latin American bishops at Medellín.[6]

Only four years after his encyclical on human development Paul VI issued another document which contributed significantly to the teaching of the Catholic Church on matters of social justice. The new document was called *Octogesima Adveniens*, to indicate that it came on the eightieth anniversary of Leo XIII's original social encyclical *Rerum Novarum*. Pope Paul took this opportunity to address some of the issues that had been the concern of the Latin American bishops at Medellín. One of the most valuable elements in his document is the way in which it acknowledges that *economic* problems often call for *political* solutions (Nos. 46 and 47); this statement can be taken as an encouragement to Christians to become involved in the political struggle for social justice. A further important point in the document is the pope's acceptance that it may not be possible for him as pope to put forward a unified message and 'solution' which will have universal validity (No. 4); in different regions the local Church may have to work out proposals which will vary from one region to another. Both of these points may be seen as a tentative endorsement of the approach adopted by the Latin American bishops, and even, perhaps, as an invitation to Church leaders in other countries to do something similar in their own situations.

The third important document on justice to come from Rome after the Council is called *Justice in the World*. It came, not from the pope, but from the Synod of bishops which took place in Rome in 1971. It is perhaps the clearest and most forthright statement on justice ever to have come from Rome. It can be seen as a positive response by these representatives of the bishops from all over the world to the stance taken by the Latin Americans at Medellín. The document contains a fundamental statement about the relationship between Christian faith and action for justice. Despite the contorted syntax of this statement, the truth it proclaimed is so important that its words have been quoted almost *ad nauseam* ever since:

> Action on behalf of justice and participation in the transformation of the world fully appear to us as a constitutive dimension of the preaching of the Gospel. . . . (No. 6)

This synod document also contains a very strong and specific commitment to justice within the Church itself; I have referred to this towards the end of chapter 1 above.

In 1975 Pope Paul issued a further document which makes a valuable contribution to the social teaching of the Catholic Church. It was called *Evangelii Nuntiandi* ('Evangelisation in the Modern World'). A notable aspect of this document is its wholehearted acceptance of the word 'liberation' and the careful and comprehensive account which its gives of the meaning of that word.

John Paul II

I want now to refer briefly to the contribution to the social agenda made by Pope John Paul II. In my opinion, his main achievement has been not so much to add some new items to the agenda (though he has done that also) but rather to offer a coherent and rounded framework for social ethics. He has proposed an integral Christian-humanistic vision of human development.[7] In this context he has made a valuable contribution by his careful theological development of the notion of solidarity. For him, solidarity is a virtue which enables people to overcome distrust and to collaborate in the creation of international justice and peace.[8]

John Paul's analysis of the nature of work and of the human person as a worker is a very important contribution to social teaching.[9] There is little doubt that his encyclical on work represents an adoption into official Catholic teaching of some of the major insights of Marxism; at the same time the pope is careful to distance himself from the notion of class warfare.

In the major addresses given on his international journeys Pope John Paul has emphasised human rights—paying particular attention to cultural and religious rights, and the right to work. On various occasions he has pointed out in very strong terms the evil effects of the model of 'development' which is widely used in today's world.

The Vatican has issued two documents directly concerned with the theology of liberation. People of different outlooks interpret these in different ways; those on one side or the other tend to emphasise the passages that lend support to their own stance on this controversial issue. There can be little doubt, however, that the first of these documents is quite critical of liberation theology while the second looks on it in a much more favourable light. The very fact that two such different documents on more or less the same topic were issued in quick succession shows that there is some divergence of viewpoint even within the Vatican itself.

It is clear that at the level of *practical policy* the Vatican is moving quite strongly to minimise the influence of liberation theology in the Church, above all in Latin America. This is best understood as a determination to distance the Catholic Church from anything that might savour of Marxism or left-wing politics. At the same time, however, the pope has given strong *theological* support to the main thrust of liberation theology in so far as this insists that justice and human liberation are a major concern of Christian faith. Indeed, John Paul has increasingly been using a theological language that has its roots in liberation theology

In recent years, John Paul has begun to pay some attention to the issue of justice for women. His 1988 document on the dignity of women is notable for an elaborate analysis of the text in the Bible where the first woman is said to be a helpmate for the first man. The pope maintains that a true understanding of biblical teaching leads to the conclusion that there is a true equality between women and men. The wife is 'subject to' the husband only in the same sense as the husband is 'subject to' her; each is called to be at the service of the other.[10] Unfortunately, the full importance of this teaching has not been appreciated because people's interest has been focused very much on the strong stance taken by the pope against the ordination of women. Feminists and others argue that to deny ordination to women is

59

to deny them equality with men. But the Vatican maintains that what is at issue is not the fundamental equality of woman but an unchangeable tradition based on Christ's choice of men as his apostles.

Over the years, Pope John Paul had made some references to the ecological issue in various addresses and documents; but until recently this aspect of his social teaching was rather under-developed. The gap was bridged by the pope's message for the World Day of Peace on 1 January 1990.[11] In this document John Paul insists strongly on the close links between peace, justice and ecology:

> . . . world peace is threatened not only by the arms race, regional conflicts and continued injustices among peoples and nations, but also by lack of due *respect for nature*, by the plundering of natural resources and by a progressive decline in the quality of life.(1)

He gives the following illustrations of the relationship between ecological problems and what he calls 'structural forms of poverty'. Unjust land distribution means that farms are so small that the soil becomes exhausted; in a search for new land the farmers then cut down the forests in an uncontrolled way. This destruction of the natural heritage is also caused by the need of heavily indebted countries to increase their exports in order to service their debts.(11)

The most important aspect of this document is its attempt to provide a biblical and theological basis for ecological concern. Adam and Eve, says the pope, were called 'to share in the unfolding of God's plan of creation' (3). This call established 'a fixed relationship' between humankind and the rest of creation.

> Made in the image and likeness of God, Adam and Eve were to have exercised their dominion over the earth (Gen 1:28) with wisdom and love. Instead, they destroyed the existing harmony *by deliberately going against the Creator's plan*, that is, by choosing sin. (3)

A consequence of this was that the earth was in 'rebellion' against humanity (cf. Gen 3:17-19; 4:12). All of creation became subject to futility, waiting to be set free together with all the children of God (cf. Rom 8:20-21).

Particularly noteworthy in the theology of this document is the pope's explicit statement that there is 'an integrity to creation' (7). What this means is that the universe has a harmony; it is 'a "cosmos" endowed with its own integrity, its own internal, dynamic balance' (8). The pope insists that this order must be respected (8). In fact he sees this as a 'fundamental underlying principle' which, for him, is intimately linked to, and in a sense part of, the principle of 'respect for life' (7). In speaking of respect for life, John Paul obviously has *human* life in mind above all. He suggests that environmental pollution and the reckless exploitation of natural resources are ultimately to the disadvantage of humankind (7).

It would seem that the pope is proposing two major grounds for respecting the integrity of creation: (a) failure to do so is a rejection of God's plan for creation; (b) failure to do so is ultimately an attack on humans. This is helpful; but it still leaves some doubt about the fundamental basis of our duty to respect non-human life and nature itself. It is evident that for the pope the intrinsic harmony and order of nature is a value in its own right; but it remains unclear to what extent this value imposes a moral obligation on humans not to interfere with the pattern of nature.[12]

The US Bishops

Among the more important advances in Catholic social thinking and teaching in recent years is the remarkable contribution made by the bishops of the USA. In 1983 they issued a joint pastoral letter entitled *The Challenge of Peace: God's Promise and Our Response*. In the second of their four drafts of this document they pointed out quite strongly the unacceptable aspects of the current conception of nuclear deterrence. However, this provoked a lot of opposition, both within the USA and, more particularly, in the Vatican. It was out of line with the view of Pope John Paul II that deterrence could be considered acceptable if it were seen as a step on the way to progressive disarmament. So, in the final draft of the US bishops' document, the idea of deterrence was not condemned.[13]

The peace pastoral was followed in 1986 by another joint pastoral of the US bishops: *Economic Justice for all: Pastoral Letter on Catholic Social Teaching and the U.S. Economy*. Like the letter

61

on peace, this document went through several drafts; and the final text was a compromise. Its criticism of the prevailing capitalist model was strong enough to enrage the conservatives but not strong enough to satisfy those who wanted something more radical. But the document represents a worthwhile attempt to criticise and assess capitalist society in the light of Catholic social teaching.

More recently the US bishops have been working to prepare a joint pastoral letter on the role of women; and, as I write a second draft document has been issued. This topic is even more difficult than the previous ones, since most feminists and many other women are angry about the treatment of women by the official Church. But the attempt at dialogue is continuing. What is particularly important in this, and in the preparation of the earlier pastorals, is the *process* which has been adopted. In each case, many formal and informal consultations are held and a number of drafts of the pastoral letter are circulated widely and discussed in great depth before the definitive document is issued. In this way a real effort has been made to ensure that the documents take account of the views and convictions of a very wide range both of 'experts' and of committed Christians. One result is that the preparation of these pastorals has been an exercise in participation and an educative process not merely for the bishops themselves but for active Christians throughout the country.

Another important contribution to Catholic social teaching and thinking was made by the final document issued by the Basel Conference of 1989 on the topic 'Peace with Justice for the Whole of Creation'. This conference was organised under the joint sponsorship of the Conference of European Churches (Protestants, Anglicans and Orthodox) and the Council of European (Catholic) Bishops' Conferences. In so far as the document is an authoritative statement from the European Catholic bishops it can be seen as a contribution to Catholic social teaching. However, the initiative for the conference came originally from the other Churches as part of their preparation for the 1990 World Convocation organised by the World Council of Churches on the theme 'Justice, Peace and the Integrity of Creation' (a convocation held in Seoul, Korea in March 1990). So it seems more appropriate to treat it in the next chapter in which I explore the development of social teaching of the World Council of Churches.

3

Social Justice and the World Council of Churches[1]

THERE IS such a wide variety of Christian Churches in the world that it is very difficult to say anything that is both true and useful about them all. In order to reduce the task to more manageable proportions I intend here to concentrate mainly on the World Council of Churches (WCC). The membership of this body includes most of the main Protestant Churches, apart from some very conservative ones which refused to join or withdrew on the grounds that the WCC had become too 'liberal' or too political or too ecumenical (in the sense of adopting a more Catholic position). Membership of the WCC is not confined to Protestant Churches. The Eastern Orthodox Churches are prominent members. So too are the Churches of the Anglican Communion which embrace Catholic elements as well as Protestant ones. Furthermore, there are now some member Churches which are perhaps more pentecostal and/or 'prophetic' than 'Protestant' in the traditional sense.

The World Council was not formally set up until 1948, so I propose to take a brief look first at what might be called the pre-history of the WCC. About a hundred years ago most of the Protestant Churches were, like the Roman Catholic Church, very much inclined to give support to the State in the promotion of order in society. There was frequently a tacit alliance between Church and State—a trade-off in which Churches were allowed to play a privileged role in society in return for recognising that the authority of the government came from God. (A few minority Churches in the Anabaptist tradition took a much more critical-prophetic stance—and suffered for it.)

In several of the Protestant Churches in the late nineteenth century there was somewhat more openness than in the Catholic Church to modern scientific developments of all kinds. Ironically, this trend left many of these Churches with a blind spot in relation to social issues. It is true that there were prophetic people, such as the great Anglican theologian F. D. Maurice, who spoke out strongly against the social injustices of modern society. But these voices were not easily heard by people who had swallowed the myth of scientific progress— a 'progress' that subjected poor workers to the harsh working of the so-called scientific law of supply and demand.

Social Commitment

In the English-speaking world in the early nineteenth century the Methodists, the evangelical wing of the Anglicans, and others in the 'evangelical' tradition, had played a leading role in campaigning for the abolition of slavery. Their concern for the most oppressed sectors of society continued long after slavery was officially abolished. Shocked by the appalling conditions which industrial workers and miners had to endure, evangelical Christians helped workers to challenge these injustices. Some of the early trade unions were organised in the 'chapels' of these Christians—so much so that even today the local branches of some unions still call themselves 'chapels'.

In the early years of the present century there was a certain convergence between this tradition of Christian social concern and the 'liberal' Protestant outlook. The result was the 'Social Gospel Movement' which aimed to transform society in a manner inspired directly by the Gospel. It flourished above all in North America, under the influence of the preacher Walter Rauschenbusch; but it was also fairly widespread in Europe.

Just after the First World War, Karl Barth launched a forceful attack on liberal Protestantism—and his challenge was remarkably successful, far beyond the boundaries of his own Church. Insisting on the utter transcendence of God and the uniqueness of the Christian faith, Barth helped Protestants to avoid reducing Christianity to liberal democracy, or to a humanised version of capitalism, or even to 'Christian socialism'. But the very success of Barth's challenge to liberal Christianity made it more difficult for the Protestant Churches to develop a coherent body of social teaching. Theologians and Church leaders who accepted Barth's sharp contrast between Christian faith and mere human religion were bound to have doubts about the rightness—or even the

64

possibility—of developing a body of social principles; to them that would sound too much like humanism or rationalism.

On the other hand the influence of Barth was very strong in a major development of the socio-political agenda of one segment of German Protestantism shortly after Hitler came to power. Some of the Church leaders refused to accept the attempt of the Nazi regime to control the Churches. In 1934 they came together as 'The Confessing Church', and issued the famous Barmen Declaration in which they proclaimed that the Church is subject to the authority of the Word of God, rather than to any State authority. One of the most significant figures in the Confessing Church was Dietrich Bonhoeffer who was later imprisoned and eventually executed by the Nazis for resistance to the regime.

It is more than fifty years since The Confessing Church came into existence; yet the attitude it represents is as relevant and controversial today as it was then. The Barmen Declaration provides inspiration for Christians who feel called to resist oppressive regimes today. For instance, *The Kairos Document*,[2] issued in 1985 by 150 leading theologians in South Africa, continues in the Barmen tradition of protest against abuse of State power. So, too, do many of the Church groups in North America who protest against the involvement of the US government in Central America. And, in 1986, Ulrich Duchrow, a leading member of the Evangelical Church in Germany, caused quite a stir with his book *Global Economy: A Confessional Issue for the Churches?*[3] In this book he argued forcefully that the Churches of the West today should dissociate themselves from the economic activities of 'the West' in much the same way as the Christians of the 'Confessing Church' distanced themselves from the Nazi regime.

Many of the Protestant Churches had abandoned or minimised the medieval emphasis on natural law, and had come to rely much more on the Bible. This made it more difficult for them to develop the kind of sophisticated social ethics that is required when society is undergoing major social changes. However, the Anglicans had preserved a good deal of the natural law tradition. It is not surprising, then, that they played a major role in the development of social ethics. Working out of this tradition, the Anglican archbishop William Temple played a large part in deve-loping the notion of 'middle axioms'. This was the name given to certain guidelines or criteria that could be used for evaluating economic or social systems. The term *'middle* axioms' was used because these guidelines were neither so universal as general moral principles nor so limited as practical moral decisions.

A somewhat different but equally important contribution to social theology was made by another key figure within the Protestantism of the time—the theologian Reinhold Niebuhr. He brought to America the richness of the European tradition but developed there a theology that avoided the naïve optimism of liberal Protestantism and the simplicities of 'the social gospel' while calling for deep social commitment.

The Oxford Conference

If we look at the Churches which are now linked in the World Council of Churches we find that in general the development of Christian social ethics is more 'linear' and less subject to the sharp swings that took place over the years in the Catholic Church. The main reason for this is that authority is more diffuse in these Churches, not focused on one person. Until very recent times the key role in the development of social teaching in the Roman Catholic Church was played by the various popes. In the other Churches, by contrast, new social thinking permeated not merely from 'the top' downward, but more particularly from the bottom upward. In this process, theologians have had a lot of influence—more so at times than the official Church authorities. This was especially the case in the years prior to the establishment of the World Council of Churches. Once the WCC had come into being in 1948 its leadership began to gain a notable degree of moral authority, especially on social issues.

A turning-point in the development of Christian social teaching was a meeting of theologians, economists and political scientists who came together in the Oxford Conference of 1937 on 'Church, Community, and State'. This Oxford meeting was a precursor of the WCC. It carried a special authority because its participants were drawn from a wide variety of Christian traditions. (But there were some notable gaps: few women took part; theologians from the Roman Catholic and Russian Orthodox Churches were absent; Third World Christians were scarcely represented; and the Nazi regime refused to allow the

66

German participants to come to Oxford—though their written contributions were available.)

One of the most important aspects of the meeting in Oxford was the way in which it brought theologians into effective dialogue with scientists and policy-makers. Thus an air of realism was introduced into the documents issued by the participants. They avoided 'the kind of ecclesiastical pontification and moralising on social and economic issues which had so often in the past characterised the churches' thought and action'.[4] This set a model for future collaboration in approaching ethical issues of all kinds. (It must be said that the Roman Catholic Church was much slower in committing itself to such an approach. It was only at Vatican II that this more open model of dialogue came to be accepted by Catholics. In the decades since the Council, the Vatican seems to have slipped back to an older model; but, as I noted in the previous chapter, the dialogue approach has been used very effectively by the bishops of the USA in preparing their joint pastoral letters on social issues.)

The Oxford Conference was important both for the approach it adopted and for the specific teaching it proposed. Its approach was to steer a middle way between general principles and detailed moral prescriptions, making use of 'middle axioms' (to which I referred above). One of the more significant criteria for authentic social action proposed by the Conference report was *nondiscrimination*. This was particularly relevant at the time, in view of the racialism of the Nazi regime in Germany. Racialism, however, did not end with the Nazis; and the World Council of Churches has remained true to the insights of Oxford in continuing to make racialism one of its major concerns right up to the present day.

Another important criterion put forward by the Oxford Conference was responsible *stewardship* of the resources of the Earth. In calling Christians to care for the Earth, the Oxford Conference was far ahead of its time; another thirty years were to pass before this issue came to the fore again.

At Oxford, the participants had very different views about the relative values and defects of socialism and capitalism. Some believed that the capitalist model could be reformed to make it compatible with Christian faith; others felt it had to be replaced with some form of socialism.[5] There was agreement that in

67

practice both capitalism and communism left ordinary people helpless in the face of an irresponsible use of economic or political power.

On the issue of war and peace the report of the Oxford Conference succeeded in combining a very strong condemnation of war as fundamentally evil, with an admission that nevertheless war might sometimes be justified as the lesser of two evils. The report focused its attention on the general question of whether any war could be justified. It recognised that different Christians take very different options: some believe that pacifism is the only authentically Christian stance; others adopt some form of the 'just war' theology; while others start from the presupposition that the State is entitled to demand that the citizen go to war to defend it, but acknowledge that in certain rare circumstances the Christian may rightly disobey it.[6] The report paid little attention to the main issue that arises today—namely, the *means* used in waging war (e.g. weapons of mass destruction, and the targeting of non-combatants).

From Amsterdam to New Delhi

The World Council of Churches came into existence in Amsterdam in 1948, eleven years after the Oxford Conference. In between, the Second World War had convulsed the world; and the horrors of the Nazi 'final solution' of the 'Jewish problem' had been revealed. No wonder, then, that the theme chosen for the inaugural assembly of the WCC was 'The Responsible Society'.

In general, the social teaching that emerged from this Assembly was very much in continuity with what had come out of the Oxford Conference. Amsterdam offered a set of criteria by which Christians might judge the extent to which any particular society was in conformity with Christian values. Such a society was obliged to work out a balance of freedom, order, and justice.[7] These were the criteria which would enable Christians to identify 'The Responsible Society'. They are still useful today. But looking back to 1948 we can now see that the whole approach was unduly Western, in both the ecclesiastical and the political senses.

From an ecclesiastical point of view, the young Churches of the non-Western world played only a minor role in the Amsterdam Assembly; furthermore, the Assembly did not concern itself very much with the question of economic development, which was of paramount interest to the peoples of Asia, Africa, and Latin America. Politically, most of the delegates had picked up some of the 'cold war' attitudes that prevailed at that time in the West. There were, however, significant exceptions. Professor Hromadka from Prague disagreed strongly with the anti-communism of the American Secretary of State, John Foster Dulles.[8] And Karl Barth had already insisted trenchantly that Christians had no reason to support the West any more than Russia.[9]

One notable feature of this Assembly was a certain humility which characterised its statements. This is seen in the way it acknowledged that the Churches themselves have contributed to social problems, by giving religious sanction to the privileged position of certain dominant classes, races, and political groups. In speaking about communism, the Assembly report acknowledged that Christians have been involved in economic injustice; this has led the working-class to believe that the Churches are against them or indifferent to their plight, and in this way it has contributed to the spread of communism.

The Amsterdam Assembly insisted that the right of ownership is not unconditional. It has to be curtailed and distributed in accordance with the requirements of justice.

The next Assembly of the WCC was held in Evanston in 1954. It had a bigger and more effective representation from what we now call the Third World; and it addressed itself more to their concerns, particularly to the question of economic development—including its international aspects In general, it helped to widen the concept of 'the responsible society', extending its largely Western sense to cover a greater measure of universality.

The Evanston Assembly insisted strongly on what we now call 'structural justice'. It recognised that 'the responsible society' does not come about simply by a change of attitude on the part of individuals; changes have to be *embodied* in political institutions. (This was the kind of emphasis which came to the fore in Catholic teaching seventeen years later, in Paul VI's document *Octogesima Adveniens*.)

Another valuable feature of the teaching of the Evanston Assembly was its warning against 'the temptation to succumb to anti-communist hysteria and the danger of self-righteous assurance concerning the political and social systems of the West.'

69

The Third Assembly of the WCC took place in 1961 in New Delhi. Among the highlights of its teaching were the following:
—A more sophisticated understanding of what it means for the Churches to commit themselves fully to authentic human development and to exploring new forms of service; for instance, an awareness that it may call for involvement in adult education rather than in schools, and in local health clinics rather than large hospitals.
—A more nuanced approach to the question of relationships with the State and secular groups; at times there is need for close collaboration, while at other times the Church may have to play a more challenging role, even at the cost of coming into conflict with the State.
—Emphasis on the ministry of reconciliation, and especially on the overcoming of racism.[10]

Geneva to Nairobi

In 1966 the WCC convened a major conference in Geneva with the theme, 'Christians in the Technical and Social Revolutions of our Time'. The conference took place within a few months of the final session of Vatican II where the leaders of the Catholic Church had attempted to deal with much the same issues in the document *Gaudium et Spes*—'The Church in the Modern World'. Some of the Catholic theologians of Vatican II took part in the Geneva Conference as well. Technically they were observers; but in fact they played quite an active role in this WCC conference (just as the observers from other Churches had done at Vatican II). So 1965-6 marked a crucial stage in the convergence of the WCC and the Roman Catholic Church on social questions.

The key word in the theme of the Geneva Conference was 'revolutions'. It is significant that there is reference to two revolutions; for there was a serious attempt to address both (i) the issue of rapid economic development which is linked to major technological breakthroughs, and (ii) the issue of social and political revolution, especially in the Third World. It is clear that Third World concerns were taken very seriously at the Geneva Conference; the pressure for this had been building up since 1948, and by 1966 the theologians from the young Churches were strong and articulate. Many of those gathered in Geneva

70

were hoping that the Church would adopt a position on 'the just revolution' parallel to the teaching on 'the just war' (between States).

The Geneva report addressed the issues of revolution and consciousness-raising which were skirted at Vatican II. Some influential Church leaders felt that in this report the WCC went perhaps too far on the question for revolution. So the stance of the Geneva Conference was reviewed a little more cautiously at a consultation organised by the WCC in a Russian monastery at Zagorsk in 1968.

It is useful to compare the stance of WCC conferences around this time with that of the Catholic Church. Both the WCC and the Catholic Church were, of course, strongly in favour of peaceful rather than violent change. Both recognised, however, that there might be very special circumstances which would justify the Christian in taking part in a violent revolution. The views of those who felt compelled to turn to revolution were treated somewhat more sympathetically at this time by the WCC than by leaders of the Catholic Church. This reflects the fact that 'liberationist' voices from the Third World were being listened to by the WCC a good deal earlier than by the Vatican. On the other hand, when Catholic Latin America 'woke up' theologically in 1968 (at Medellín) this new voice was so loud and so articulate and so obviously Christian—that it was quickly noticed by Christians from all Churches and in every continent. Indeed it soon became 'a sign of contradiction' which led to new alliances and new divisions among Christians—and these cut right across the older denominational divide.

The Geneva Conference helped to lessen the polarisation that had taken place between those who favoured capitalism and those who opted for socialism. Instead of simply comparing capitalism with communism it spoke of three systems—free enterprise, mixed economy, and state ownership. The participants concluded that each of these systems was compatible with the Christian faith. The role of Christians, they said, was to be 'critical participants' in the societies within which they found themselves.

The WCC and the Pontifical Commission for Justice and Peace established and jointly sponsored 'The Committee on Society, Development, and Peace' (SODEPAX), which held its first conference in Beruit in 1968 on the issue of world development. It is interesting to note that it was at another SODEPAX consultation a little later, that Gustavo Gutiérrez, the first of the 'liberation theologians', provided material which became the basis for his book, *The Theology of Liberation*. Unfortunately, the activities of SODEPAX were curtailed by the Vatican in the early 1970s (presumably because it was acting too independently); eventually it was allowed to die. Since then, cooperation between Rome and the WCC has not been at all easy—even though the agendas each has been addressing have been very similar.

Meanwhile, the Fourth Assembly of the WCC took place at Uppsala in 1968. That was an extraordinary year: there was war in Vietnam and Nigeria, and major tension in the middle East; in Europe and North America there was the rapid spread of Maoist ideas among young people, and in the universities there were student 'revolutions'. In Latin America there was oppression, simmering unrest, and a continued movement towards revolution. At this very time the Churches were beginning to see themselves and be seen by others as champions of the oppressed. And there was rapid growth of cooperation 'in the field' between the major Churches on social issues. The Assembly tried to respond to the crises of the times. Perhaps its most striking statement is that 'Christ takes the side of the poor and oppressed'.

But more significant than any statement of the Assembly was a certain change of emphasis that followed from it—a move from a *study* orientation to 'action programmes.' This was spearheaded by the activist Eugene Carson Blake who had become General Secretary of the WCC in 1966.[11] The most significant and controversial of the new 'action programmes' was the 'Programme to Combat Racism' (PCR), established in southern Africa. This gave rise to considerable unease among many of the more conservative Churches, and some withdrew from the WCC. But, on the other hand, the moral support given by the WCC to liberation movements has been of major importance—and not merely for these movements but also for the WCC itself and its member Churches.

Late in 1975 the fifth Assembly of the WCC was held in Nairobi. The percentage of voting delegates who were women had increased from 9 per cent at Uppsala to 22 per cent at Nairobi. No wonder then that the role of women in the Church

72

and in society was one of its major issues. So too was the ecological question, which at this time was beginning to have a much higher profile on the social justice agenda of many committed Christians. It was around this time that Christians in WCC circles began to replace the phrase 'The Responsible Society' with one that spelled out much more specifically the kind of society which the Christian is called to work for, namely, *'a just, participatory, and sustainable society'*.

Recent Times

The next Assembly of the WCC took place in Vancouver in 1983. Although it represented no radically new departure, it gave an indication of more recent concerns and some significant shifts of emphasis. As before, racism was an issue, with Desmond Tutu and Allan Boesak as outspoken critics of the South African apartheid system. In the face of this and other instances of structural injustice there was some tension between the activist-liberationist people and those who preferred a 'softly, softly' approach.

As on previous occasions, there was a certain tension between the Churches of 'the West' and those of the Third World. Ecology and the nuclear threat were major concerns of those who came from the West; on the other hand, unjust international economic relationships and structures, and forced underdevelopment, seemed to be more pressing issues for Christians from the poorer parts of the world. Some of the latter group were inclined to dismiss the peace issue as a First World 'luxury'; and they were afraid that ecological concern might be used to restrict economic development in Third World countries.

However, the representatives from the Pacific area helped to bridge the gap between the Third World and the First World. They shared the concerns of other Third World people. But they were also very concerned both about ecology and about nuclear weapons (which are tested in the Pacific); this gave them a common cause with activists from Europe and North America. Indeed at this Assembly the Christians from the Pacific made a very valuable contribution to the vision and stance of the WCC as a whole.

At about this time the WCC phrase 'a just, participatory, and sustainable society' was replaced by another, even more compre-

73

hensive, one. The new formula was '*Justice, Peace and the Integrity of Creation*'. This expresses very well the three key elements in the social agenda of *all* the mainline Churches today.

In the years following 1983 the WCC and its member Churches continued the work of promoting 'justice, peace and the integrity of creation', in preparation for the next major WCC Assembly in Canberra in 1991. An important contribution to Christian thinking about peace was made in 1986 by a 'pastoral letter and foundation document' issued by the United Methodist Council of Bishops in the USA. This statement echoed many of the ideas of the joint pastoral letter of the Catholic bishops of the USA which had been issued three years earlier.[12] However, as one might have expected from the Methodists, it is somewhat more effective in its treatment of the biblical foundation for Christian teaching on peace. For instance, it suggests that to rely on atomic weapons for deterrence is to engage in 'nuclear idolatry'; to do so would mean usurping the sovereignty of God over all nations and peoples. So the Methodist pastoral letter takes a stronger stance against the holding of nuclear weapons than that taken by the American Catholic bishops' pastoral.

A further major step in the development of Christian teaching on social issues was that taken by the European Ecumenical Assembly in Basel in May 1989 under the joint sponsorship of the Conference of European Churches and the Council of European (Catholic) Bishops' Conferences. The theme of the Assembly was 'Peace with Justice'. It issued a very inspiring final statement under the title 'Peace with Justice for the Whole of Creation'.[13] In view of the fact that it covers the present social justice agenda both comprehensively and specifically I propose to give a broad outline of the whole document and to focus attention on some of its more significant points.

'Peace with Justice for the Whole of Creation'
The first major section of the document is entitled 'The Challenges we Face'. It lists threats to justice, threats to peace, and threats to the environment (9-13). It goes on to stress how these all interlock with each other; for instance, the problems of deforestation, of refugees, of population explosion, and of oppression of women and children are very complex because in each of them major issues of justice, peace, and environment are linked

74

together (14–17). The authors then refer to the deeper roots of the current crisis of our world. They note that the problems of modern society stem from the abuse of technology. This in turn arises as a result of 'an ideology of constant growth without reference to ethical values'. The document says: 'As Christians, we cannot uncritically advocate an ideology of human progress which of itself does not take adequate account of the whole person' (18-20).

The next section of the document is entitled 'The Faith we Affirm'. Among the striking points in this section is its account of the biblical notion of *shalom*, a word that 'embraces the gifts of justice, peace and the integrity of creation in their mutual interrelation' (29). There is also a strong emphasis on Christ's renunciation of violence, which is presented as a challenge to the Christian (32). Perhaps the most important point in this section of the document is the insistence that while God has given to humanity the task of being *stewards* of creation, this does not give us the right to *dominate* creation for our own ends: 'Stewardship is not ownership' (33).

The next section of the document is entitled 'Confession of Sin and Conversion to God'. It includes some remarkable admissions, e.g. 'We have caused wars and . . . have condoned and often too easily justified wars'; 'We have failed by regarding Europe as the centre of the world and regarding ourselves as superior to other parts of the world' (43). The authors then go on to spell out in a very concrete and moving way what is involved today in being converted to God. Among the things that have to be got rid of they mention: 'the heritage of antisemitism in our societies and churches', the refusal to recognise the gifts given to women in the life and decision-making processes of the churches', and 'a life-style and . . . ways of production which violate nature' (45). They also speak out against 'the marginalisation of the 'Two Thirds World'. The authors use the phrase 'Two Thirds World' to describe the countries of 'the South' which are often called the 'Third World'. They made this change in language because some people take exception to the phrase 'the Third World'; and also because the phrase 'the Two Thirds World' provides a more accurate and graphic description of these countries.

The heading of the next section of the document is 'Towards a Vision of Europe'. It is very topical, suggesting various practical ways in which justice, peace and the integrity of creation can be fostered. Indeed, its proposals are so topical that some of the hopes it puts forward have already been overtaken by the development which took place in Eastern Europe in the months following the Basel Assembly. The authors of the document were quite prophetic (in both senses of that word) when they issued this strong plea:

> In the process of transformation which Europe is now going through, countries, groups and people will be under the temptation to give absolute priority to their own interests, . . . If this happens, the limited room for rapid change may be used up very soon. We plead: let this process of transformation be also a *process of reconciliation.* . . . (62)

This section of the document also acknowledges that minority peoples within Europe have the right to resist assimilation into the dominant cultures (63; cf. 86g). But the authors also make the strong statement: 'There are no situations in our countries or on our continent in which violence is required or justified' (61).

The final section of the document proposes a long series of very practical affirmations, commitments and recommendations. One of the more interesting contributions here is the new language it introduces; the document commits the participants to work for 'an international economic order . . . an international environment order, . . . an international peace order' (72, 74, 75). In earlier writings it had been customary to call for 'a new international economic order'; by omitting the word 'new' from this phrase, the authors bring out clearly that what exists in the world today is not really an economic *order* at all, but rather a *disordered* system where the weak are victims of the strong. This section of the document also includes clear proposals on a variety of topical issues, e.g.

—Debt: Write off the debts of the poorest countries and alleviate the burden on all; change the policies of the International Monetary Fund (84b).

—South Africa: Institute a trade embargo as proposed by Church leaders there (84e).

—Women: Improve decisively the involvement of women in decision-making processes in the Church, to ensure that women

76

are equally represented in Church bodies and theological faculties (84j).

—Environment: A 'complete reversal of the concept of sustained economic growth' (87a).

—Energy consumption: Reduce by 50% the *per capita* energy consumption in industrialised countries (87d).

—Life-style: Adopt a style of living that damages the environment as little as possible (87j).

One of the most important points to note about this Basel document is that it is fully ecumenical. It comes out of an assembly held under the joint sponsorship of the Conference of European Churches and the Council of European (Catholic) Bishops' Conferences. The delegates there represented all the major Churches of Europe, and most of the minor ones. The fact that they could agree on such a concrete and detailed document shows just how much common ground exists between the Churches today. The document comes up with clear and strong consensus statements even on issues which might have been expected to split Protestants, Catholics, and Orthodox— the thorny issues of the population problem (84f), the protection of unborn life (84g) and the role of women in Church decision-making (45 and 85j). All in all the Final Document of the Basel Assembly is one of the most significant and moving articulations of the social agenda of the Churches in our time. The challenge for Christians is to ensure that it will become widely known and be taken seriously by Christians everywhere.

The Seoul Convocation

In March 1990 there took place in Seoul, Korea, a 'World Convocation' on the topic 'Justice, Peace and the Integrity of Creation' (or JPIC as this subject has come to be called). The convocation was convened by the World Council of Churches. The Vatican refused the invitation of the WCC to co-sponsor the meeting; it did, however, send a delegation of twenty official consultants—and many other Roman Catholics were present either as observers or as members of delegations from national Councils of Churches. The purpose of the convocation was not simply to explore the topic but to invite Churches to commit themselves solemnly to the promotion of justice, peace and the integrity of creation. The meeting was seen as a major step towards fulfilling the mandate of the WCC Vancouver Assembly of 1983 and a preparation for the next General Assembly of the WCC in Canberra, Australia in 1991.

The draft document brought before this World Convocation was itself the result of an elaborate process of consultation and re-drafting.[14] It is an impressive document. The major part of it is an exposition of a set of grave problems facing the world today—an account prepared as background material for discussion to take place before the convocation, and in work groups at the convocation itself. This draft text is an authoritative and valuable document in its own right. Successive sections of it outline the realities of our world, under the headings of injustice, violence, and the disintegration of creation. The problems are graphically illustrated by personal accounts of the difficulties that people experience. The document goes on to show how the problems relating to injustice, lack of peace, and the degradation of the environment are all linked together and interrelated. It points out that at the root of the different threats to life is an unjust world economic order (66). This in turn is linked to the misuse of science and technology to gain power over nature and over others (69). Ultimately, the crisis is a spiritual one (72); it springs from 'the modern mindset'—a set of 'attitudes, goals and values that have been ages in the making.' (68)

The remaining parts of the draft document contain proposals for a set of major 'affirmations' to be issued by the convocation and for a set of 'covenants' to be entered into by the participants. These parts of the material were worked over very thoroughly by the delegates and observers during the days of the convocation, and adapted quite significantly by them.

The final document issued by the convocation is a very important contribution to the stance of the Churches in relation to issues of justice, peace and ecology.[15] A major part of the document puts forward a series of affirmations or professions of faith and acts of commitment:

—Firstly, 'we affirm that all forms of human power and authority are subject to God and accountable to people.' This formulation brings together in a very effective way two central points—that those who wield power are accountable to God and that they are answerable to *the people* on whose behalf they exercise authority. It leads on to an insistence on the right of people to full participation. It is followed by a commitment to support people's movements in their struggle for human dignity and liberation, and in their struggle to achieve just and participatory forms of government and economic structures.

—Secondly, 'we affirm God's preferential option for the poor and state that as Christians our duty is to embrace God's action in the struggles of the poor in the liberation of us all'. A point to note here is that the phrase 'God's preferential option for the poor' was inserted into the final document in place of the somewhat weaker text in the draft document—'God's particular love for the poor' (143). It is also noteworthy that the convocation recognises God's action in the liberation struggles of the poor.

—Thirdly, 'we affirm that people of every race, caste and ethnic group are of equal value.' The draft text has said that they are of equal value *before God* (144). The omission of the words 'before God' actually strengthens the statement.

—Fourthly, 'we affirm that male and female are created in the image of God'. This leads on to a commitment to 'resist structures of patriarchy which perpetuate violence against women in their homes and in a society which has exploited their labour and sexuality'. There is also a commitment to resist 'all structures of dominance which exclude the theological and spiritual contributions of women and deny their participation in decision-making processes in church and society'. This text involves some significant modifications in the text of the draft document. In referring to the Church, the final text seems to have toned down somewhat the strongly feminist position put forward in the draft document. It uses the phrase 'structures of dominance' rather than 'structures of patriarchy'; and it omits the words 'full and equal' which, in the draft text, had been before the word 'participation'. It also omits the statement that God is 'both father and mother to all' (145). Nevertheless, the statement remains a sharp rejection of sexism in the Church.

—Fifthly, 'we affirm that access to truth and education, information and means of communication are basic human rights.' The emphasis on education is an addition to the draft text; and another new element is a commitment to seeking to ensure that other faiths besides the Christian one will be represented accurately and respectfully in the media.

79

—Sixthly, 'we affirm the full meaning of God's peace. . . . We will resist doctrines and systems of security based on the use of, and deterrence by, all weapons of mass destruction, and military invasions, interventions and occupations.' This strong statement represents a significant shift towards a position that is much more pacifist than had been previously held—and more pacifist than the current Vatican position.

—Seventhly, 'we affirm that the world, as God's handiwork, has its own inherent integrity. . . . We will resist the claim that anything in creation is merely a resource for human exploitation.' The statement leads on to a commitment to be members of 'the living community of creation in which we are but one species'. This, too, is a very strong statement, one that goes far beyond what was proposed in the draft document. Not only does it affirm the integrity of creation but it also puts forward a very strict criterion for judging the extent to which humans can interfere with the pattern of nature: we are just one species among many and we must respect the other species who together with us form the community of creation. The text also includes an acknowledgment of, and repentance for, the misuse of the biblical statement 'to have dominion' and 'subdue the earth'. It is interesting to note that the text no longer uses the notion of human 'stewardship' of the earth; instead it says that people have a special responsibility as *servants* to care for creation; and it suggests that in doing so we reflect God's creating and sustaining love.

—Eighthly, 'we affirm that the land belongs to God.' This affirmation is followed by a commitment 'to join in solidarity with indigenous communities struggling for their cultures, spirituality, rights to land and sea; with peasants, poor farmers and seasonal agricultural workers seeking land reform; and to have reverence for the ecological space of other living creatures.' This remarkable statement links together in a beautiful and effective way the issue of justice for the poor and the issue of ecology. It is particularly helpful to be reminded of the inseparable connection between the struggle of indigenous peoples for their land and their struggle to retain their culture and spirituality.

—Ninthly, 'we affirm the dignity of children'. This affirmation is a new one, which was not in the draft document. The participants felt the need to advert specifically to both the problems which face the younger generation and to the contribution they can make and are making to the building of a new society.

—Finally, 'we affirm that human rights are God-given and that their promotion and protection are essential for freedom, justice and peace.' Like the previous affirmation, this too is an addition to the original draft text. The statement includes an admission that the 'churches have not been in the forefront of the defence of human rights'. A point to note is a stress on the right of people with disabilities to be fully integrated into the community.

The document then goes on to put forward four acts of covenanting. The first of these is for a just economic order and liberation from the bondage of foreign debt. The second is for the true security of all nations and people, for the demilitarisation of international relations, against militarism and national security doctrines and systems and for a culture of non-violence as a force for change and liberation. The third act of covenanting is for preserving the gift of the Earth's atmosphere and to nurture and sustain the world's life; for building a culture that can live in harmony with creation's integrity; and for combating the causes and destructive changes to the atmosphere which threaten to disrupt the Earth's climate and create widespread suffering. The fourth covenant act is for the eradication of racism and discrimination—and for the dismantling of the economic, political and social patterns of behaviour that perpetuate racism.

The document as a whole is a powerful statement of the Christian understanding of our call to work for justice and peace and for the protection of the fabric of nature. It is both inspiring and practical. Perhaps its most important contribution is the extent to which it succeeds in *integrating* the social justice agenda of the Church, so that this agenda is no longer a list of loosely connected items but a single fabric in which justice, peace and care for the earth are inseparably woven together. Christians can see here what is involved today in working for social justice.

Polarisation

Here I want to note two developments—one hopeful and the other very disturbing—which have been taking place in the past couple of decades mainly among Third World Christians. The hopeful development is the growing convergence between different versions of liberation theology and spirituality in widely

81

separated parts of the world. This is a movement which would probably have taken place in any case, but it has been greatly facilitated by an organisation called the Ecumenical Association of Third World Theologians (EATWOT). This association is not under the sponsorship of any single Church or council of Churches. Rather it brings together committed theologians from many different Churches, and the organising group has a balance of Catholic and Protestant members. The various conferences organised by EATWOT have helped theologians facing very different situations in various sectors of the Third World to learn from each other; they have also fostered a deep dialogue and convergence between feminist theology and a variety of Third World theologies; and EATWOT has challenged and encouraged those theologians in the First World who have been struggling to develop an alternative spirituality and theology, challenging the complacency and 'respectability' of Christians and Churches in the Western world.[16]

The more disturbing recent development is the rapid expansion of a fundamentalist, sometimes pentecostalist, version of Christianity especially in countries where there is gross oppression and major social upheaval. The sects involved are not members of the WCC; in fact they are in sharp conflict with its values and approach. There is no doubt that a lot of money is being channeled into the promotion of this escapist type of Christianity. The money comes partly from conservative Christian groups, mainly in North America. But there is little doubt that some of the money is also coming from *politically* right-wing bodies—such as the South African government, and security agencies of various countries. Their aim is to counter the growing commitment of Christians to the struggle for liberation. Their success in spreading a 'de-politicised' version of Christianity is a major concern not only for liberation-oriented Church people but even for cautious middle-of-the-road Church leaders. In the face of this challenge, socially conscious Christians have become more determined than ever to overcome the outdated divisions inherited from past centuries and to work together to tackle the pressing issues of justice and peace in the world today.

4

Old and New Principles of Justice and Peace

IN THIS CHAPTER I propose to list various principles which sum up the official teaching of the Catholic Church on different aspects of justice and peace. There is little difference at present between this teaching and that of the other Churches. Yet, I have decided that it is best to confine myself here to Catholic principles. I shall not attempt to make a similar list of principles to encapsulate the teaching of the Orthodox, Protestant, or Anglican Churches. These Churches do not generally seek to be quite so explicit and specific in presenting principles and so it does not seem appropriate to try to fit them into this more 'Catholic' mode.

Before giving the list of principles I want to explain why it is useful to have such a list. There was a tendency in the past to see the list of principles as providing a rule book which would be a *basis* for pastoral action. Our task was simply to apply the rules to each situation as it arose. I would prefer to see the principles as emerging as a *result* of pastoral action. They sum up the conclusions that have emerged in a process of action-reflection-action-reflection. Their main purpose is to be a crystallisation of the different values that we, and the rest of the community, have discovered to be operative in our Christian response to the various situations of injustice and lack of peace in which we have found ourselves.

It can be useful, as we face decisions about our actions in the future, to have this kind of concrete articulation of principles in relation to justice and peace issues. First of all, it helps us to be *consistent* in our commitment. For instance, I might realise that in my struggle to overcome some glaring economic injustice I have failed to pay sufficient attention to other values which I also strongly believe in—perhaps the value of allowing others to participate in decision-making, or the value of respect for another culture. The list of principles helps me to have an integrated and balanced approach, rather than whirling erratically from one value to another as each comes to my attention.

Having a list of clearly formulated principles may also help people to avoid another kind of inconsistency—a lack of coherence between their professed beliefs and the way they behave in practice. For instance, a group of clergy composed exclusively of men might experience some embarrassment if they find themselves preaching about the principle that women have equal rights with men. Similarly, in a racially mixed area, a group made up exclusively of white people will feel challenged by their own words if they find themselves proclaiming the principle of the equal rights all races. In such cases the articulation of the principle could make people aware that they themselves may not be doing enough to promote the rights they affirm.

I am presenting here two lists of principles concerned with justice and peace. The first list represents my understanding of the Catholic Church's teaching as it developed up to about 1960. The second list is my attempt to give expression to the new teaching that has emerged since that time. If this were a purely historical study I would present each of the two lists separately. But my intention in this chapter is to help the reader to understand the present-day principles more thoroughly. So I shall match the two lists with each other, taking each principle in turn and comparing the older version of it with the new version. In this way I hope to bring out the development that has taken over the past generation. As I go through the list I shall comment briefly on each of the old and new items, filling in some of the background and indicating how each item is a response to a particular historical situation.

Principle No. 1: Older Version: The dignity of each individual human person must be respected and defended; and the individual must not be subordinated to the State.

> COMMENT: This principle represents a defence of the individual against collectivism and State absolutism.

Principle No. 1: New Version: The dignity of each human person is to be respected and this is shown in practice by respecting his or her fundamental human rights; many of these rights can be

84

specified e.g. the right to life, to security, to work, to a family income, to the ownership of property; the right to freedom of conscience; the right to have one's culture respected; the right not to be discriminated against on the basis of gender, race, wealth, or social status; and, particularly, the right to participate in the making of all decisions which affect one's life and the life of the community.

COMMENT: The re-formulation of this principle involves considerable modification. There is now far more emphasis on human rights, and the list of such specified rights has been getting longer. Fundamental rights are linked to human dignity, so that respect for these basic rights becomes the test for whether human dignity is being respected. The new formulation of the principle does not mention the State specifically. This is because the State is just one of a variety of potential aggressors against human dignity and rights.

Principle No. 2: Older Version: The individual has a right to own private property.

COMMENT: This second principle was also intended as a defence of the individual against collectivism. But in practice the right to private property came to be seen as the central principle of the Church's social teaching; individuals and systems were judged in terms of how strongly they supported this right. The inevitable result was that the Church found itself allied with the property-owning and conservative sectors of society and very much out of sympathy with reforming groups or with anybody who had any leaning towards socialism.

Principle No. 2: New Version: Humans are the stewards of the goods of the Earth and have a duty to respect them and use them for the benefit of all; the right of every individual to own private property is, in practice, a necessary but not a sufficient means of putting this principle into effect.

COMMENT: In the revision of this principle the right to private property has been put into context and relativised. There have been, and still are, tribal societies where there is little ownership of private property, or at least of immovable property such as land. The right to own private property is a practical necessity in the Western world; it is the only

85

effective way in which the dignity of the person can be safeguarded. But it is not an absolute; it takes second place to the right of all people to benefit from the goods of the Earth. (In regard to the duty to respect the goods of the Earth see principle no. 16 below.)

Principle No. 3: Older Version: Society is not just a collection of isolated individuals; it is, rather, an organic whole, a community composed of diverse elements where all are called to cooperate together for the common good.

COMMENT: This principle represents the Church's rejection of individualism; by insisting on the organic unity of society the Church provided a basis for its demand that those who have power and wealth should respect and care for the less privileged sectors of society.

Principle No. 3: New Version: Society is not just a collection of isolated individuals; it is, rather, a community composed of diverse elements where all are called to be in solidarity with each other and to cooperate together for the common good.

COMMENT: The main thrust of this item remains as before but the important notion of 'solidarity' now replaces that of 'organic unity'. This latter phrase is a metaphor borrowed from biology; so it is inadequate to express the complexity of a human community where each individual is sacred. The word 'solidarity' has a specifically human connotation to it; it suggests that the members of a human community are linked together by their own deliberate choice as well as by bonds of common origin. In the light of the Church's response to the reality of global unity we now need to add a further principle at this point, namely:

Principle No. 3a (New): The primary community is the human race taken as a whole rather than individual nations.

COMMENT: The point here is that our responsibility for others is not confined to the local or national level but extends to people everywhere. To fail to recognise this in our present-day world is to put the very survival of our world at risk.

Principle No. 4 Older Version: The authorities in society have the God-given task of promoting the common good and they have a God-given right to the obedience of the citizens.

COMMENT: This principle is an instance of the attempt made in Church teaching to avoid the extremes of individualism on the one hand and collectivism on the other. The notion of 'the common good' is very fundamental in Catholic social teaching. But it is almost impossible to specify its exact content. It does *not* mean merely 'the greatest benefits for as many people as possible' since that might involve sacrificing the good of a small number of people for the benefit of the majority. The notion of 'the common good' implies that the welfare of the community as a whole is promoted; so it presupposes the organic unity of society (principle no. 3). Another point in this principle no. 4 is worth noting: the Church was not content to offer a purely secular basis for the authority of the State; God is brought in to provide the foundation for the authority of secular governments—and to lend weight to both their rights and their duties.

Principle No. 4: New Version: The authorities in society have a sacred duty to promote the common good and they have a right to the obedience of the citizens.

COMMENT: The changes here have more to do with the tone of the statement than its meaning. The new version speaks of a 'sacred duty' of authorities to promote the common good, whereas in the older version the reference to God was more explicit. Church teaching would still understand human authority to be derived ultimately from God. But nowadays the position is rather more nuanced. This is because we now have a more sophisticated understanding of the autonomy of the secular world and, within it, of the political sphere. Consequently, Church leaders and theologians are more likely to speak of the rights and duties of citizens and rulers as *moral* and political matters than as overtly religious ones. There is need also to add an extra principle at this point, namely No. 4a:

Principle No. 4a (New): The common good of all people cannot be attained when the government of any individual country single-mindedly pursues the national interest of that country without taking due account of the welfare of the people of other countries; the common welfare is to be promoted by cooperation under the auspices of international agencies such as those of the United Nations family.

COMMENT: This principle arises from a practical application of principle no. 3a (about the unity of the human community) and principle no. 4 (about the common good). The point is that international cooperation is now a pressing moral obligation. For our world has become a single economic entity, where decisions taken in major stock markets, board rooms, or government offices affect people everywhere. Furthermore, the quality of human life, and even its very survival are now threatened by weapons of mass destruction and the use of atomic reactors, by environmental degradation, and by the irresponsible using up of scarce mineral and energy resources. So now it is not just citizens but also governments that have the duty of respecting a higher authority; they must use and respect the international agencies—and work to make them more effective and more just.

Principle No. 5: Older Version: The common good of society required that the State respect the principle of subsidiarity. This means that authority is to be exercised as far as possible at a lower level rather than a higher level. So, professional organisations and local and regional authorities are to have a high degree of autonomy, subject only to monitoring by the State in the interests of the common good.

COMMENT: This principle of subsidiarity was considered to be an important and distinctive feature of Catholic social teaching. If it were properly implemented then the extremes of State absolutism and irresponsible individualism would be avoided. However, the principle is just a very general guideline. In order to implement it in practice, one would have to spell out the values that the State is to safeguard. In the past, Church authorities were not very helpful in laying down the criteria to be used in judging the extent to which the State may intervene in the activities of professional organisations or local authorities, in the interests of the common good. There was a tendency to assume that, in general, the less the

88

State intervened the better, but the need for some intervention to protect the poor was affirmed.

Principle No. 5: New Version: The common good of society requires that all agencies—political, social, and economic—respect the principle of subsidiarity. This means that responsibility is to be exercised as far as possible at a lower level rather than a higher level. However, the common good requires that there be monitoring agencies at every level, from the local up to the international level, to ensure that abuses are minimised.

COMMENT: In this revised version the principle of subsidiarity is applied much more widely than before. It has become clear in recent times that people become alienated when they find that the major decisions which affect their lives are made by people with whom they have little personal contact. This applies perhaps above all in the economic sphere. For instance, a board of directors, meeting in New York, may decide to close down a factory at the other side of the world, taking little account of the workers. Church teaching would favour the 'small is beautiful' approach, as giving a more human dimension to life and work. In fact Ernst Schumacher, the pioneer of this approach, was deeply influenced by the insistence in traditional Church teaching on the principle of subsidiarity.[1] Among the values that should be taken into account in deciding the scale of operations are the following:

(*a*) personal responsibility and involvement by people in decisions that affect their lives in the political, economic, social, cultural or religious spheres;

(*b*) a sense of community and solidarity with those who share one's life and work;

(*c*) ecological responsibility, e.g. using local food and materials as far as possible, not making use of inappropriate technology, not squandering energy or mineral or food resources, and not polluting the environment.

There is another small but significant difference between the older and the new version of this principle: the international dimension is taken into account. The present situation requires a twofold movement away from the older emphasis on the nation-State. On the one hand, some of the authority exercised in the past by the State must now be passed *upward* to inter-

89

national agencies. On the other hand, some of it must be passed *downward* to regional or local authorities.

Principle No. 6: Older Version: Those who hold power in society must show particular concern for the poor and other categories of people who are vulnerable to exploitation; those who have wealth and influence must renounce exploitative practices and attitudes; governments have the duty of modifying systems or mechanisms that foster injustice by giving undue power to certain groups.

COMMENT: This principle spells out some very important implications of the older version of principle no. 3 above: since society is understood to be an organic whole, the stronger sectors cannot disclaim responsibility for the weaker sectors. In practice this means that authorities at all levels must provide certain safeguards to ensure that those who are vulnerable are not exploited.

Principle No. 6: New Version: Those who hold power in society must show particular concern for the poor and other categories of people who are vulnerable to exploitation; those who have wealth and influence must renounce exploitative practices and attitudes; governments and international agencies must ensure that structural injustices are eliminated.

COMMENT: There is a significant change in the wording here (even though the meaning has changed very little). The useful phrase 'structural injustice' now replaces the more cumbersome formulation used previously. Structural injustice arises when one nation, race, class, gender, group, or individual has undue and unchecked power and is therefore in a position to take advantage over others. Individuals who act justly in their personal relationships may well be involved in operating political or economic mechanisms that are structurally unjust— e.g. a legal system might be biased against the poor, and international trading agreements are often biased against countries that produce primary products such as tin, cocoa, and sugarcane. The above revised principle no. 6 now has to be supplemented by two new principles to which I give the numbers 6a and 6b;

90

Principle No. 6a (New): The special concern of the Church for those who are disadvantaged or oppressed in any way is to be shown by the making of a 'preferential but not exclusive option for the poor'.

COMMENT: This principle refers specifically to the role of the Church. The most significant word in it is, of course, the word 'option', which is something much more than mere 'concern'. It means, firstly, that the Church and its leaders repudiate any political or social alliance with those who unjustly hold power or privilege in society. Secondly, it means that Church leaders, and the Christian community as a whole, are called to be in solidarity with all categories of people who are underprivileged in any way. These include people who are treated unjustly because of their race, or gender, or sexual orientation; people who suffer from some bodily or mental disability, and people who are economically poor, or at a disadvantage in the political, social, cultural, or religious spheres. Being in solidarity with these groups, the Church will go on to defend their interests, and to work effectively for the kind of structural changes that will eliminate such systematic injustice; this applies at the global, national, and local levels.

Principle No. 6b (New): The Church, which seeks to promote justice and a true peace based on justice, must itself give clear witness to these values in its own institutions and procedures.

COMMENT. There is a negative and a positive aspect involved here. Negatively, the Church accepts that it is obliged to eliminate structural injustice that may have crept into its institutional life. Positively, the Church is obliged to establish traditions and institutions that respect the dignity and responsibility of the person and that foster dialogue and participation at all levels of Church life. Furthermore, since the Church is committed to promoting and witnessing to true peace based on justice, it must ensure that its own institutions provide just and effective ways of resolving disputes and of responding to complaints. At times this will involve the use of full legal procedures; at other times it will be appropriate to introduce less cumbersome forms of 'due process', e.g. agreed procedures for arbitration and mediation.

Principle No. 7: Older Version: The State has the duty of check-ing abuses and promoting order and equity in the economic sphere. But the common good of society is best attained when the State refrains as far as possible from direct involvement in economic affairs. It should concentrate on providing a political environment within which individuals and groups can engage responsibly in 'free enterprise' in the economic sphere, and in voluntary activities to alleviate social problems.

COMMENT: This principle, perhaps more than any of the others, conveys something of the particular character and flavour of Catholic social teaching during the first half of the twentieth century. The Church rejected the philosophy and practice of uncontrolled individualism. But it was also strongly opposed to the development of a large State bureaucracy which would control every facet of people's lives, for it believed that would involve undue interference in the rights of the individual. Church authorities offered one practical guideline to the State in its attempt to keep the balance: 'Stick to political matters and keep out of economic affairs as far as possible'. There was some wisdom in this advice; but with the development of the modern economic system the distinction between politics and economics became very tenuous. Any modern government which aims or claims to keep out of economic affairs is in fact making a political decision that has major economic implications!

Principle No. 7: New Version: The State has the duty of checking abuses and promoting order and equity in the economic sphere. This requires careful monitoring and decisive political action designed to ensure that the openings for exploitation are mini-mised. At times the State itself may become involved in directly economic activity; the principle of subsidiarity will indicate when this is appropriate.

COMMENT: The main change is the clear recognition that what happens in the sphere of economics is largely determined by political decisions. This implies an acknowledgment that the State must play a major role in economic affairs. Never-theless, the new formulation of the principle retains a key element of the older version: it seeks to avoid *excessive* inter-vention by the State and the consequent bureaucratisation of life. So the principle of subsidiarity is involved again.

Principle No. 8: Older Version: Society should be organised in a way that ensures that class struggle is avoided. The ideal way to achieve this is for the State to be organised on 'corporative' or 'vocational' lines, where a particular 'corporation' represents all those involved at any level (owners, managers, workers) in a given economic activity (e.g. agriculture, transport, etc).

COMMENT: Condemnation of class warfare is one of the most consistent features of Catholic social teaching over the past century. However, this older version of principle no. 8 went much further than such a condemnation. It aimed to eliminate or minimise the possibility of class struggle. It proposed a 'blueprint' for a just society which would replace the old class-ridden structure. The new society was to be structured into various sectors along vocational or corporatist lines, so that the interests of people would no longer be identified with others of the same class but rather with others in the same sector. (See my account of this approach in chapter 2 above.)

Principle No. 8: New Version: Society should be structured in a way that allows for dialogue between its different sectors and does not foster polarisation between classes or other groupings. This can take place under any one of a variety of socio-political and economic systems. No one of these systems is proposed by the Church as the best. In view of the wide variation from one part of the world to another the Church cannot advocate one system as having universal validity; but the Church can put forward certain values and principles as criteria for evaluating the various options that arise in any particular place. In choosing a particular system people should not allow themselves to be deceived by the use of language. For instance, 'public ownership' of various economic enterprises may be a deceptive title—since it may refer to a kind of 'state capitalism' which leaves real power concentrated in the hands of a relatively small managerial group. Similarly, a 'free enterprise system' may in practice be one that concentrates power unduly in the hands of a few.

COMMENT: The major change here is the recognition that the Church does not have a 'blueprint' for the ideal society. What the Church has to offer is not a system but certain values and principles that must be respected in any system that claims to be truly human. A second important change is the recognition of the need for local Church leaders to evaluate and respond to the local situation. This implies that a system that is appropriate for one country or continent may be unsuitable for another. The note of caution about the deceptive use of language is based on the Pope John Paul II's perceptive and sharp critique (in his encyclical on human work) of both the capitalist ideology of the West and the Marxist ideology of the East.

Principle No. 9: Older Version: Workers have the right to form trade unions to represent them in negotiations with their employer as they seek just wages and decent working conditions; under certain conditions workers have, as a last resort, the right to go on strike in pursuit of these demands.

COMMENT: Note that the purpose of a trade union was understood to be confined to the defence of the economic rights of its members vis-à-vis the owners and management of the company where they worked.

Principle No. 9: New Version: Workers have the right to form trade unions to help them defend their vital interests. These interests include the immediate economic ones such as just wages and humane working conditions. But they also include the rights of workers in a more general sense. So trade unions may legitimately become involved in negotiations about the general economic policies and structures of society (e.g. who controls the means of production and the way in which use is made of the resources of the society—and even of the world as a whole). While being involved in such broadly political issues, trade unions should avoid too close involvement in 'party politics'. The strike weapon may be used as a last resort in struggling for justice; but it should not be used as an instrument of 'party politics'.

COMMENT: There is a very notable change here. The Church was very slow t acknowledge the right of trade unions to become involved in political matters—presumably for fear that this would foment class struggle. However, Pope John Paul II, with his keen interest in the Polish 'Solidarity' union, could appreciate how closely economic and political matters are intertwined so in his encyclical 'On Human Work' he laid down the guidelines summarised above.

Principle No. 10: Older Version: A worker who is head of a family is entitled to a family wage. Mothers of families should not normally work outside the home.

COMMENT: With the industrial revolution, work in industry and business began to replace farm and craft work as the main type of work in the Western world. Work was no longer a family affair. The wage-earner was commonly a man—or at least it was widely assumed in official Church circles that the 'normal' wage-earner was a man. In these circumstances many Church leaders began to insist that 'the woman's place is in the home', and that consequently the wages of the man ought to be at least sufficient to keep the whole family in frugal comfort.

Principle No. 10: New Version: Every family is entitled to an income sufficient to meet its basic needs and to provide some security for its future. In order to provide this income it may be necessary to organise society in such a way that the State or some other agency supplements the income of those members of the family whose wages are insufficient. Family income should be adequate to ensure that it is not necessary for *both* parents of young families to leave the home each day to go out and work. There should be practical (economic/financial) recognition that caring lovingly for children in the home is real and valuable work. Those who take on this task—usually women—should not be penalised economically for doing so. The various professions and others spheres of work are to be organised in a way that does not put women at a disadvantage, especially those women who choose to devote time to child-bearing and caring for young families.

COMMENT: The change is considerable. First of all, the new formulation is more realistic about the sources for a family income. But the most important changes concern the role of women in work. There is an insistence that the home-making work done by most women (and some men) is real work and should be valued and rewarded like other forms of work. It is no longer assumed that women should not go out to work. But at the same time women should not be forced to fit into an economic system which grew up catering mainly for the needs of men; so the special needs and rights of women in the

95

field of work are to be respected. This new teaching is to be found in Pope John Paul's encyclical on work (19).

Principle No. 11: Older Version: Schemes should be designed and implemented to allow workers some share in the profits of the firms which employ them—and some voice in their management as well.

COMMENT: This principle represents a way of tempering the evil effects of the capitalist system. The proposal to give workers a share in profits and even some 'say' in management was put forward quite strongly by Pius XI as part of his radical critique of capitalism. (As I noted in chapter 2, Pius XII was more reluctant to challenge the dominant economic model of Western society.) So the demand for a share in profits and management might be seen more as an expression of an ideal of the older Catholic social teaching than as an immediate demand.

Principle No. 11: New Version: The dignity of the human person is very closely related to the character of the person as a worker. It is mainly through our work that we are called to exercise our role as stewards of creation, protecting and ennobling nature; in this way we act in the image of God the creator. Work should be of a kind that enables people to find personal fulfilment in it. Though it may at times involve toil, work is basically good and necessary for humans. The fundamental basis for determining the value of work is not the usefulness of the object produced but the fact that the one doing the work is a human person. Therefore the worker must never be treated as a mere instrument of production. Human work must not be treated as a mere commodity, to be sold and brought in accordance with 'the law of supply and demand'. Technology is to be used as an instrument at the service of workers; so it must not be allowed to enslave people or deprive them of the right to work. Labour takes priority over capital and the two are not to be set in opposition to each other; capital is itself very largely an embodiment of human work. In view of these basic truths about human work the most obvious practical conclusion is that the human person has a fundamental right to work. Therefore it is not sufficient to offer unemployment benefit to those who have no work; that is acceptable for a transitional period, but it does not meet the basic human need for work. Furthermore, the work to which everybody in society has a right must not be mere drudgery but creative, fulfilling work. Finally, in view of the fact that work is normally the joint enterprise of a number of people, it follows that workers are entitled to share both in the profits that are the result of their labour and in any decision-making that will affect them as workers.

COMMENT: The major change here is that a whole theology of work has entered into Church teaching—mainly through Pope John Paul's encyclical on work. At the practical level there is now an urgent need to insist on the right to work. The further claim that workers have a right to share in profits and decision-making is made firmly in the Vatican II document on 'The Church in the Modern World' (68).

Principle No. 12: Older Version: Citizens have a right and duty to use lawful means to resist serious misuse of power by a government.

COMMENT: This principle represents 'the bottom line' in the older Catholic teaching in support of the individual in the face of an excessive and oppressive exercise of power by governments. There was some lack of clarity about what would constitute an *unlawful* means. In general it was taken that the State had the right to decide what means were unlawful. This, of course, put a very severe limit on the extent to which the citizen could resist the misuse of power by the State.

Principle No. 12: New Version: Oppressed groups and all citizens have a right and a duty to work by lawful means for the replacement of any government which notably and consistently fails to respect fundamental human rights.

COMMENT: The change here is mainly one of emphasis; specific mention is made of the right of those at the bottom of society to claim their rights and to work for justice. Until recently the Church teaching tended to play this down. In the past, when Church leaders called for a more just society, they directed their challenge mainly to those with power, rather than to the powerless and the marginalised. Church people were reluctant to encourage those at the bottom of society to struggle for justice because that might lead to civil disorder; and there was a tendency to give a higher priority to order and stability than to justice. Another point to note about the revised version of this principle is that it makes specific mention of fundamental human rights. Respect for human rights is a practical criterion for judging whether or not a government is misusing its power. Perhaps the most important point to note does not concern the words used in the formulation of the principle but rather how the words are now interpreted: the phrase 'lawful means' is no longer given such a restricted meaning as in the past. There is some recognition of the fact that certain edicts of a very repressive government might be so grossly unjust that they would not in fact be lawful; they might lack the minimum requirements of true law.

Principle No. 13: Older Version: Sedition or violent resistance to an existing government is unjustified.

COMMENT: In view of the Church teaching that the authority of governments comes from God, it is not at all surprising that sedition should be condemned. But what is of particular interest is to note that towards the end of the last century and during the early years of the present century *all* violent resistance to a duly constituted government was understood to be seditious and therefore wrong. The medieval teaching on the right to resist a tyrannical ruler had been abandoned, at least in practice.

Principle No. 13: New Version: Sedition or violent resistance to an existing government is almost invariably unjustified.

COMMENT: The new formulation is almost the same as the old one; however, a small but important phrase—'almost invariably'—has been added before the word 'unjustified'. The point is that the Church recognises that in principle it is possible to have a justified war of liberation. However, it teaches that in practice such violence would almost certainly do more harm than good; normally, therefore, other forms of resistance must be used instead.

Principle No. 14: Older Version: Under certain stringent conditions a State is entitled to go to war against another State, in defence of its legitimate interests.

COMMENT: The Church had a well worked out teaching about 'the just war', i.e. the conditions under which a State would be entitled to defend itself by violent means. This teaching represented a careful combination of moral elements and pragmatic ones. Moral elements: war could not be justified unless there were a just cause and unless the means used were justified (e.g. no deliberate attack on non-combatants). Pragmatic elements: war could not be justified unless there was a reasonable hope of success; and neither could it be justified if the harm it involved was greater than the evil it set out to remedy. At the heart of this pragmatic aspect of the teaching about war lies the moral concept of 'proportion': it is wrong to pursue any cause if doing so causes disproportionate harm.

Principle No. 14: New Version: (i): The development of international institutions and the nature of modern warfare make it highly unlikely that a war between States, or an armed rebellion by the citizens of a State, could be justified. However, one cannot in principle exclude the possibility, as a last resort, of a justified recourse to armed resistance against unjust aggression or against sustained oppressive tyranny.
(ii): The use of weapons of indiscriminate mass destruction cannot be justified; and to rely indefinitely on such weapons as a deterrent is also unjustified.
(iii): There is a lack of full agreement among theologians and Church authorities about the morality of holding such weapons as a deterrent on a purely interim basis.
(iv): State authorities should respect the consciences of individuals who conscientiously renounce violence even in a just war.
COMMENT: The changes here are very considerable:
(a) The Church teaches that some of the basic elements of an international global authority have been gradually emerging; in so far as such global institutions have already emerged, their moral authority transcends that of individual States; consequently the arbitration and peace-making efforts of these international agencies impose morally binding obligations on State governments.
(b) The principles governing war between States are now seen to apply also to armed resistance from within a State to a tyrannical regime.

(c) It could not be morally justified actually to fire the weapons that are currently targeted on major population centres, since that would involve the deliberate killing of innumerable non-combatants.

(d) Pope John Paul II and some other Christian leaders and theologians seem to be saying that it is legitimate and even necessary for nations to hold on to such weapons, on an interim basis, so long as they are making use of the breathing-space this provides to engage in serious disarmament negotiations. Other Christians leaders and theologians believe that the threat or intention to use immoral weapons is itself immoral and that the holding of such weapons as a deterrent cannot be justified at all; for they could only be credible as a deterrent if various military 'field-officers' have clear instructions to use them under certain circumstances and if they have the serious intention of doing so.

(e) For a long time the Church refused to accept the right of anybody to be a conscientious objector; but Vatican II acknowledged this right in its document 'The Church in the Modern World'.

New Principles

In addition to the reformulated principles outlined on the preceding pages the new list of principles on justice and peace must now include two further items—nos. 15 and 16, below. These deal with matters scarcely thought about in the past.

Principle No. 15 (New): All people and all peoples have a fundamental right to integral human development. The model of development chosen must be one that lessens rather than widens the gap between the privileged and the under-privileged in the economic, social, sexual, political, and cultural spheres.

COMMENT: Within the past generation the idea of economic development has come to the fore; this has led on to a wider and more integral conception of human development in all spheres. The Church now teaches that such an integral development is a basic right both for humanity as a whole and also for each ethnic-cultural group. In principle, development offers the possibility of eliminating the terrible disparities in wealth, power, and status that mar our world. In practice,

100

however, these disparities have been made much greater by the type of development that has been chosen or imposed. The Church now challenges such misdevelopment.

Principle No. 16 (New): The style of development allowed and fostered by governments must be one that respects the integrity of creation and is sustainable.

COMMENT: The concepts of sustainability and respect for the integrity of creation are ideas that have burst on to the justice and peace agenda within the past twenty years. They involve three aspects:

(a) We are stealing from future generations if we use up the resources of the earth faster than nature renews them—unless we make compensation, or use them in a way that will be of value in the future.

(b) We are destroying the quality of present human life if we do not organise our industry, agriculture and life-style in a way that is ecologically responsible.

(c) We are called to see ourselves as part of nature and to live in respectful, peaceful and harmonious partnership with all other creatures. There is no general agreement as yet on all that this involves. Not many Christian moralists or constitutional lawyers would claim that animals, plants and nature itself have 'rights' in the full moral sense—though there are indications in very recent times of a significant move in that direction.[2] There is general agreement that we humans are obliged to avoid an exploitative attitude towards our partners in creation—the animals and plants of the Earth—and towards the inanimate world. This means, at a minimum, that we are obliged to avoid inflicting unnecessary pain on animals. However, in our treatment of living but non-human creatures it is not yet clear what criteria should be used to distinguish between necessary pain and needless cruelty. And few of the theologians or leaders of the main Churches have even begun to address seriously the moral issues surrounding the treatment of animals in modern factory farming.[3] It is also generally accepted that we have a moral obligation to ensure that the variety of species of animals and plants is respected. But once again it is not clear what this means in practice— what limits it puts on human interference with nature. Finally,

101

it is accepted that humans may not destroy or wantonly pollute the environment; but as yet there are no generally accepted practical criteria for applying this general guideline.

The Key Principles

Having completed the list of principles, old and new, I want to point out that in each of the two lists there are one or two items which from a practical point of view assume a central importance. In the old list it is no. 2—the right to private property. Many Church leaders and theologians tended to allow this principle to play a dominant role in the social teaching of the Church; and the result was that other principles (which we now see as more important) were undervalued in practice.

In the revised list the emphasis has shifted very considerably. The Church is now more obviously concerned about the plight of poor and powerless people rather than about the rights of property owners. So in the new list of principles a crucially important point is contained in the new version of principle no. 1—the right to participate in decision-making. If Christians today are looking for a convenient yardstick by which to tell whether justice is effectively present in a given situation then they should ask: 'Is real responsibility being exercised by the people affected by the decisions being made; are they allowed to share in the decision-making?' If people have the right to share in making the decisions that affect their lives, then they are in a position to ensure that their other basic rights will be respected, and that true justice and peace will prevail.

Within the past few years, Christians have been coming to see that an equally crucial point is that expressed in the new principles no. 15 and no. 16 above: the need for a new model of human development—one that promotes an integral and balanced progress for all people and peoples, a development that is ecologically sensitive and viable, and that enables humans to live in partnership with nature; without this there is no long-term future for humanity. This is a point to which I shall return in chapter 6.

102

PART THREE

What the Church Can Do

5

The Church's Option

THE TEACHING of the Church on matters of justice and peace is an important contribution to the promotion of social justice in the world. But many people—Christians and non-Christians—feel that teaching is not sufficient. They ask, what can the official or institutional Church actually *do* about the various issues covered in the previous chapters. In this chapter I want to respond to this question.

In the first chapter of this book I outlined various items of 'the social justice agenda', e.g. the gap between rich and poor, international debt, oppression and liberation, racism, injustice against women, the infringement of human rights, and the plight of refugees. Over the past twenty years very many Church leaders have come to recognise the need to go beyond preaching and teaching about such issues. They feel called to act—to make what they call 'a preferential option for the poor'.[1] This means committing themselves and the official Church to take a very clear stand on the side of the victims of poverty, oppression, debt or exploitation.

Presuppositions

To make an option for the poor involves (as the word itself indicates) making a choice. As a first step in exploring this choice I want to examine its presuppositions. The option is an act of faith which only makes sense in the context of a particular way of interpreting the world. It presupposes that we see the world as a battlefield where the many little struggles we face each day are part of a much more comprehensive confrontation between the forces of good and the forces of evil. This is not something that can be taken for granted. Many people choose to believe that the world is not such a bad place, that though we all have our ups and downs, things work out all right for people in the end. Expressed crudely in this way, such a view sounds incredibly naïve; but a lot of people in the Western world today seem to live by this view in practice—at least so long as they are dealing with the suffering of others rather than their own!

Christians accept that there is a clash between good and evil in society. But not very many of them have come to think of this as a struggle between sin and grace, between the forces of evil and the power of God. And if they do occasionally think of it in these terms they seldom see this as central to their own journey towards God. In recent years this has begun to change. Theologians now stress that sin and grace are not just spiritual or personal realities. They have a public or political aspect—if we have eyes to see it. So the struggle between sin and salvation is not confined to some inner world, to the personal, spiritual-psychological sphere. It is fought out in the economic and political world and in the cultural and ecclesiastical spheres as well. In fact it coincides to a considerable extent with the major conflict of interest in our world between oppressed and marginalised groups on the one hand and oppressive forces on the other.

Of course, most Christians are well aware that the world of politics, economics and culture is bad in many ways and in need of transformation. But very many 'good' Christians cannot think of any significant contribution they could make towards this transformation; consequently they do not see it as a major religious issue for themselves. They conclude that what God wants of them is to do their best, *within the given structures*, to live a 'good' life. So they try not to introduce new abuses into public life, and to be as kindly and generous as possible to the people they have to deal with. But they are not seriously trying to change the world. For them the main thrust of their Christian vocation concerns their private and domestic lives, rather than such public matters as economics, politics, culture, and organised religion.

What happens when the question arises about the need for a change in the structures? Private citizens generally see this as the task of the politicians or other public figures. On the other hand, many politicians and people who hold public office see themselves as compelled to work within the existing structures which have been accepted, at least tacitly, by the ordinary people. So, to a large extent, neither group takes responsibility for the evils of the world; each leaves the task of transforming society to others—or to God!

106

To make an 'option for the poor' involves rejecting as quite inadequate these approaches to life. Such an option presupposes that we interpret our world in terms of an ongoing and public struggle between good and evil. In other words, we see the main energies and forces of our world as gathered under one or other of what Ignatius Loyola called 'the two standards'—that of Jesus and that of the Evil One.[2] We understand our Christian faith as a call to be actively involved with Jesus in *saving the world*. In practice, this means commitment to changing structures, institutes and traditions which embody injustice or bring about inequity in society.

Who are the Poor?

We can represent the world as a circle divided by lines radiating from the centre (like the sections of an apple-pie); the various sectors represent the different areas of life—economic, political, socio-sexual, cultural, ecclesiastical (see diagram p. 107). In each of these sectors of life most of the real power is held by quite a limited number of people. They can be represented as being within a small circle located at the centre of the larger circle. Out around the edges of the outer circle are those who are marginalised, left powerless. In between are people with varying degrees of power in the different sectors of life. It is worth noting that those who have a lot of power in one sector usually have access to power in other sectors as well; wealth gives a person political and social 'weight' or 'clout'; and even in Church affairs the voice of the wealthy tends to carry more weight. On the other hand, those who are marginalised in one sector of life are often on the margins in other sectors as well.

To struggle against injustice means committing oneself to changing the structures of society so that there is a better distribution of power. The aim is to give effective power to those who have been left out on the margins. This involves reducing the excessive and unchecked power of those in the centres of power in the various sectors of society.

The most obvious forms of powerlessness are in the economic and political spheres—for example, not to have enough to eat, or to be tortured by security forces. When Church people in Latin America first began to use the phrase 'option for the poor' they had in mind a stand by the Church in favour of victims of this kind. This aspect of the 'option for the poor' will continue to be of central importance. But there are other sectors of life in which people come up against structural injustice. So the meaning of 'an option for the poor' has to be extended to refer to a commitment to challenge structural injustice in the socio-sexual, cultural, and ecclesiastical sectors of life as well as the political and economic sectors. For instance, women find that in business and social life most of the positions of power are held by men. And in the Church, the laity find that the clergy hold almost all the power. So women and laity are 'poor' in the theological sense; and those who are in a position to work for change are called to take their side.

There is a danger of depriving the phrase 'option for the poor' of any real challenge by extending it too widely; everybody can be understood as 'poor' in some sense. Some theologians, keenly aware of the danger, wish to restrict the notion of 'the poor' to those who are economically and politically deprived. But this is inconsistent—and it could even, at times, be a way of evading the challenge of relinquishing ecclesiastical power! The precise nature of the option each of us is called to make at any particular time depends very much on the situation in which we are living and working. In this chapter and the following one I shall focus attention on the role of the Church as a community and institution within society, leaving to the final two chapters an examination of what it means to make an option for the poor within the institutional Church itself.

To make an option for the poor is to commit oneself to resisting the injustice, oppression, exploitation and marginalisation of people which permeate almost every aspect of public life. It is a commitment to transforming society into a place where human rights and the dignity of all are respected. There are two equally crucial aspects to this commitment—an experiential aspect which can be summed up under the word 'solidarity' and a political aspect which has to do with action. I shall outline each of these in turn.

Solidarity

At the heart of the experimental aspect of an option for the poor lies a deliberate choice to enter in some degree into the world of those who are deprived—to share in a significant way in their experience of being mistreated, bypassed, or left helpless. It springs from compassion and involves a choice to deepen this compassion by sharing to some extent in the suffering of the poor. But the experience is not totally negative: by entering the world of deprived people one also begins to experience their hopes and their joys.

In practice, this aspect of option for the poor has to do with life-style. Life-style includes the kind of food we eat, the clothes we wear and the way our homes are furnished. But these are of secondary importance. Much more significant are our choices about the area in which we live, the friends we cultivate, the kinds of work we undertake and the attitudes and style we adopt in doing all these things.

In so far as one begins to share the life of disadvantaged people one begins to have that sense of togetherness which

109

frequently characterises such groups. This is the *experience* of solidarity which provides a matrix within which the *virtue* of solidarity can be developed. Without the experience of solidarity the would-be reformer cannot help thinking about the poor as 'them', the objects of my sympathy. When one thinks and feels in that way it is almost impossible to avoid being both paternalistic and manipulative—and the people will sense this, no matter how well it is disguised. It is only to the extent that a person becomes part of the group and is able to think of 'us'—and to be treated by the people as 'one of us' that this person has the possibility of becoming a truly effective and respectful agent of change.

Of course this is not an 'all or nothing' affair. The person who is making the option has probably come from a different background and may retain a different accent or even skin colour. In that sense the person may always be seen as different; but the group with whom he or she has come to live or work may choose to accept him or her as 'one of us', one who shares their interests. It is not in my power to be fully in solidarity with a particular group of deprived people; all I can do is *offer* to be in solidarity with them. And this offer is not made in words but in the attitude with which I come to them. In response they may choose to offer me the gift of solidarity, of treating me as 'one of us' (or, perhaps, 'one *with* us').[3] They make that choice in their own time and in their own degree; it is not something I can presume or demand or even hasten.

I have said that the *experience* of solidarity provides the matrix within which the *virtue* of solidarity can be developed. The virtue is a habitual attitude and approach which inclines one to be sensitive to the needs and feelings of others in the group and to devote oneself generously to the common welfare. The development of the virtue of solidarity takes place within the context of the struggle against injustice. Like other virtues, solidarity has to be constantly nourished and in two ways: firstly, one has to strive constantly to play a part in developing common policies with the other members of the group and to act on the basis of these joint policies; secondly, one must be open to challenge by other members of the group.

110

Commitment to Action

Having looked at solidarity which is the experiential aspect of an option for the poor we can now go on to the second major aspect of this option, namely, a commitment to take action to overcome structural injustice. This involves a series of steps:

—There is need first of all for a careful *analysis* of the situation to bring about an understanding of the basic sources of the injustices. Otherwise a lot of energy may be wasted in working for superficial changes without tackling the real causes of the problem.

This should lead on to a distancing of oneself from *collusion* with the groups or forces that are responsible for the injustice. For instance, a Church leader may find it necessary to refuse favours or invitations from certain politicians or business interests, lest acceptance be construed as approval of what these people or groups are doing.

—Then there is need for carefully planned and concerted action at the political level to *challenge* the injustice. It is clear that there should be a certain gradation in such action. At first there might be a private protest; if this does not succeed there might be letters to the newspapers; then, perhaps, a public protest march, and so on.

—Finally, there is need to design realistic *alternatives* to the unjust structures which are being challenged, and to begin the process of bringing these alternatives into being. For instance: suppose a large group of poor people on the outskirts of a city find they cannot afford to buy sites for their own homes; and suppose they conclude that a major reason for this difficulty is the speculation in building land by a small number of wealthy and influential people. In challenging this injustice they should have some clear alternative to propose, e.g. a government-controlled limit on the price of land, and/or a publicly-owned 'land bank', and/or very heavy tax on profits from the sale of land, etc.

In all of these steps it is very important that those who are making the option for the poor do not take it on themselves to set the agenda or to provide the answers. It is not for them to play a leading role in describing the situation, or in deciding what the major injustices are, or which of them are the most urgent, or how they should be challenged; they should not take it on themselves to organise protests against injustice, or be the

111

ones to decide on alternative structures. At each step of the way the victimised people themselves should be enabled, as far as possible, to speak and act on their own behalf. For it is only in this way that they can overcome the sense of helplessness and dependency which is a fundamental part of their situation. Those who have chosen to act in solidarity with them may have to 'hold back' for quite some time. When they do intervene it should be to facilitate the disadvantaged people themselves in coming to understand the causes of their problems and in planning effective action to overcome them.

An Option by the Church

An option for the poor is, first of all, a very personal choice, made by an *individual* committed Christian who desires to share in Christ's work of bringing salvation to the world. But that is not enough. There is need also for *communities* of committed Christians, to make such an option on behalf of the Christian institution to which they belong. In recent years this has happened fairly widely; many religious congregations and some societies of lay people (i.e. certain sectors of the St Vincent de Paul Society) have committed themselves in this way.

But even that is not sufficient. The *institutional Church* itself, at every level, faces the challenge of making an option for the poor. The way in which this can be done is to have Church leaders act on behalf of the Church as a whole, and in a manner that shows that they have the backing of most of the membership of their Churches. The Catholic bishops of Latin America at their meetings in Medellín (1968) and Puebla (1979) committed themselves very publicly to such an option. The leaders of the WCC have made a similar, though broader, commitment in dedicating themselves to 'justice, peace, and the integrity of creation'. Many other Church leaders have felt called to be in solidarity with the poor and the powerless and to join their struggle for dignity and justice. In most cases these leaders have endeavoured to make their commitment not merely in their personal capacity as Christians but also as representing the official Church—carrying as many as possible of their people with them in this option for the poor.

It is important to note this distinction between an option for the poor made by an individual or small group of Christians on

112

the one hand and, on the other hand, an option for the poor made by, or on behalf of, a whole Church, at a regional, national or international level. I have written elsewhere about what is involved when individuals or groups commit themselves to making an option for the poor.[4] So I shall focus attention here on what is involved in the official Church making such an option.

Social Analysis

When the leadership of a Church sets out to facilitate the Church in making an option for the poor the various steps outlined above have to be gone through. It is of particular importance that a serious *analysis* be made of how structural injustice operates in the particular society. This will provide a basis for avoiding *collusion* in injustice and for the *challenge* which the Church is called to make to injustice in society; it should also give some indication of the kind of *alternatives* which Church people are called to work towards. I do not propose to go into detail here in describing such a social analysis, but some comments on the topic are called for.

In recent years I have met many enthusiastic Christians who have heard of the important contribution made by social analysis to liberation theology and have come to have an idealised and nearly mythical conception of it. They seem to imagine that there is a 'tool' called 'social analysis' which, if they can get a hold of it, will provide them with an almost magical means for developing a really effective liberation theology in their own situation. This is a rather naïve view based on a misunderstanding of the real value of social analysis. The main reason for engaging in it is not to provide information that was unknown to anybody in the past. Rather it is to help oppressed people come to an understanding of who is exploiting them and how; and to have their consciousness transformed through this process of discovery.

Some degree of social analysis is necessary for those who wish to challenge injustice in a serious way. It can enable people to understand how structures of injustice come into being and how they benefit some groups and make others suffer. It is particularly helpful for poor and deprived people to come to a realisation that poverty and deprivation are not simply 'the will of God' or 'the nature of things'; only in this way can they be motivated to work against injustice. It is also important to help people to

113

direct their anger and energy towards the more fundamental causes of injustice. For instance, people who find they can no longer afford to buy sufficient food may be helped to avoid putting all the blame for this on the peasants who grow the food; instead they can come to understand that the producers and the consumers may *both* be victims of an unjust international economic system.

In my experience, the most important function of social analysis is not to come up with entirely new information but to enable 'ordinary people' to discover for themselves, and to really make their own, information that may already be known to people who have had the benefit of some general economic education. When this new *understanding* is set in the context of the daily *experience* of exploitation and oppression of ordinary people the mixture is a very powerful one. So, if I am doing a social analysis with a group of deprived people, the result should be a deeper understanding of injustice both for them and for me; but what *they* learn from the experience may be different from what *I* learn. They are likely to gain a new understanding of their situation in the sense of new knowledge about the real source of their suffering. I too am likely to gain a new understanding of the situation; in my case, however, it may not be new theoretical information but a deeper realisation of how injustice affects their lives, with some particularly dramatic instances which can bring this home to me and to others.

In some Third World situations there is an almost total lack of accessible information about who owns the wealth and power and about which groups are most deprived. The available statistics are quite outdated—and in some cases they were grossly inaccurate from the beginning. This means that those who wish to work for justice have to rely on their own efforts when they come to do a social analysis.

On the other hand, in most Western and some Third World countries economists and sociologists have produced fairly accurate and comprehensive studies of the socio-economic patterns. This information is available in highly technical reports which can be understood only by those who have some familiarity with the technical language in which they are written and with the kind of graphs and diagrams they use to communicate their findings. If such scientific studies are available, those who are

114

working for justice cannot ignore them. They must find ways of making the technical information available to ordinary people. The main challenge is not one of *teaching* in the usual sense; it is rather a matter of helping people to find an *entry-point* into this scientific world, a way of relating the information to their own experience.

One way of doing this is by a critical reading of the financial section of the daily newspapers. The journalists who write there about current economic trends have the task of presenting the scientific data in a form that is accessible to non-experts who have an interest in the topics and some familiarity with them. However, the financial section of a newspaper is very much directed at the business community. It does not take a great deal of critical analysis to see that most of the economic correspondents and journalists are writing from a particular point of view; they share and promote values that are quite opposed to the values of those who are working to overcome the structural injustice of society. It can be very enlightening to study what these journalists have to say about such topics as the sale of land for building, or how economic growth should be stimulated, or how international debts should be handled.

In this situation social analysis will include an examination of the courses of action that are being presented as 'good' and those presented as 'bad' from the point of view of the business community; this can lead on to a careful assessment of the implications of these policies for ordinary people. This kind of examination teaches people to realise that even the most scientific economic reports are seldom presented in a purely neutral way. The scientists and the reporters already have their own value system. This means that they approach the situation with a certain 'optic' or point of view. Those who have made an option for the poor have the task of unmasking that 'optic' and reinterpreting the facts from the point of view of their own commitment to the building of a just society.

Over the past twelve years I have been involved in three different projects of social analysis, with very different kinds of groups. In each case the study produced some important information that helped those involved to make decisions about how to challenge injustice and promote genuine human development. Two of the projects went a step further. They used what is called a 'listening survey', which is part of 'the psycho-social method',[5] inspired by the ideas of the Brazilian educator Paulo Freire. This led the participants to focus attention not merely on the social fabric but also on what are called 'generative issues'. This means that the analysis helped those who took part in it to identify the 'burning questions' for local people. For example, the people of one area had a strong hope that water could be piped into the area; in another area the people were very angry about corruption in the local health centre. This hope and this anger generated the energy to motivate the people to become involved in dedicated work for real change.

Even more important than the information or understanding produced by the social and cultural analysis was a *change of consciousness* which came about in the participants. The change in the local people who took part in it meant a new appreciation of their own way of life and a real determination to defend themselves and the best of their traditions against unjust interference. The change in those who came from outside to share the task of analysis with the local community meant a deep awareness of the dignity and value of the local people and a sense of the richness of their traditions; for the first time the 'outsiders' learned to stop feeling that they were the ones who had come to teach the local people how to live well; they realised that they were the ones who had most to learn.

All this shows why committed Church leaders wish to get involved in social analysis. They know that if it is done sensitively it can create a common bond between the local people and those who are trying to be in solidarity with them. But there is a further very practical reason for Church leaders to be involved in this way: in many Third World countries (and to a lesser extent in the West) those who hold the power preserve their position by making it very hard for ordinary people to find basic information about how that power is being used. It may be difficult to discover who owns certain property or industries, or who is responsible for serious ecological damage. Wherever there is a repressive government the mere fact that people begin to *look for* such information puts them in considerable danger. In these circumstances Church leaders can play a very important role by lending their authority to projects of social analysis undertaken at various levels. These may range from a local study undertaken by rural or urban workers to the much more high-powered investigation that can be done by research institutes. Where this work is done under Church auspices it is often more difficult for those in power to prevent it taking place.

Analysis of the Role of the Church

One of the most important topics that should be covered in a social analysis is the role which the Church itself has been playing in this particular society, and how the Church is perceived by the ordinary people. To bring out this point, take the case of the Anglican Church in England. In recent years its leaders have challenged the government very strongly on issues of social justice—so much so that they have provoked sharp criticism from leading politicians. Nevertheless, the Anglican Church there has by no means reached the point where it is widely seen as the champion of the poor against an uncaring government. Even if, in the future, its leaders go much further in speaking out on social issues it is unlikely that there will be any notable change in the way the Anglican Church is perceived, so long as it continues in other ways to act very visibly as part of the British establishment.

The Catholic Church in Ireland is in a rather similar situation. In recent years the Bishops' Council for Social Welfare, the Jesuit Centre for Faith and Justice, and the Justice Desk of the Conference of Major Religious Superiors have mounted a very sustained attack on government policy in relation to the poor here in Ireland, and the Bishops' overseas development agency Trócaire has been a very vocal critic of some aspects of foreign policy. Yet the Church as a whole is still seen—especially by poorer people—as part of the establishment; and its leaders still act in a way that fosters this perception. This has greatly lessened the credibility and impact of its challenge to prevailing policies and attitudes.

Perhaps the most serious temptation facing Church leaders is an unthinking assumption that they can 'run with the hare and hunt with the hounds', i.e. that they can take a strong stand on matters of social justice while still maintaining a close relationship with those who are responsible for injustice. In recent years those who hold positions of authority in the Church are coming to see that if they wish to give effective leadership in making an

117

option for the poor they must disengage themselves very clearly from any kind of collusion with those who perpetrate structural injustice. In this respect, actions speak louder than words. For instance, President Reagan visited Ireland some years ago, at a time when there was a strong reaction against the role of the United States in supporting the Contras in Nicaragua and the Marcos regime in the Philippines. None of the Irish Catholic bishops took any public part in the various receptions and events of the president's visit. Their absence was seen as very significant, especially in view of the fact that, when President Kennedy visited Ireland many years before, Church leaders had been prominent in welcoming him.

It is not easy for Church leaders to renounce privileges which offer the official Church the opportunity to be visibly present on public occasions and in the institutions of the State; for such presence may be seen as part of the incarnation of the Church in the world. That is why there is need for a clear analysis of the role of the Church in society. It can provide a solid basis for the difficult decisions that have to be made by Church leaders who wish to stand unequivocally in solidarity with disadvantaged groups at home and abroad. It can show the high price that is often paid for the privileged role given to the institutional Church and its leaders; in subtle ways they are manoeuvred into giving (or seeming to give) at least tacit support to social injustice. In order to ensure that the message the Church is sending is not compromised, its leaders may feel obliged to distance themselves from those who are responsible for injustice.

The official Church is by no means a homogeneous or monolithic reality; in many countries it is an uneven mixture of agencies or institutions that embody very different sets of values. For this reason an analysis of the role of the Church in society should attempt to answer this serious and disturbing question: which sectors of the Church are already on the side of the poor and which sectors are colluding in injustice or even promoting it?

An honest and comprehensive answer to this question will provide guidelines for policies to be adopted by Christians and Church leaders who wish to be in solidarity with the poor. They will plan ways to lend support to, and be supported by, those parts of the institutional Church that share the same values and vision. At the same time they will set out to win over, or challenge, the sectors or people that have not taken a clear stand against injustice—and, as a last resort, they will look for ways of ensuring that their own work is not blocked by such people or groups.

At first sight it may seem to be somewhat disrespectful to engage in the kind of analysis of the institutional Church which I am recommending. But in fact it can be very valuable from a religious point of view to study the Church in this way. It helps people to put a name on the uneasiness or even the anger they may be experiencing about the role in society played by some sectors of the Church; this enables them to recognise that what they are uneasy about is not the Church itself, or the Church as it should be, but something that has gone wrong within it. This in turn can set them free to identify with those parts of the institutional Church which are challenging injustice.

Challenge to Injustice

It would be pointless to try to list the various ways in which Church leaders and the official Church can challenge injustices and promote peace; for they vary according to the endless variety of concrete situations in which injustice and lack of peace arises. The most I can do here is to make a few suggestions about ways in which the Church can respond to some of the more specific items on the social justice agenda outlined in chapter 1.

International Debt: In regard to this topic the Church may appear to be rather powerless. But in fact it could contribute significantly towards a solution by a judicious use of language. Suppose Church leaders undertook a campaign to encourage people to speak about *'usury'* instead 'interest' in the case of many of the older loans on which the amount paid back in interest far exceeds the original loan. This would be an accurate description of the actual situation and it would help to make clear that to continue to demand interest in such cases is grossly unjust.

Justice for Women: In the matter of overcoming discrimination against women the Church is in a position to do quite a lot. A first and crucial step should be the elimination of sexist language from all public prayers and Church readings. For it is no exaggeration to say that to continue to use sexist language in

119

public at the present time is to pollute the moral atmosphere. This language is so offensive to many people that it blocks them from hearing the real meaning of the Word of God.

At the same time a determined effort must be made to enable women to play an equal part in decision-making in the Church. One way forward is for particular Churches to adopt, for some time, the kind of policies now practised in the WCC (e.g. there has to be an equal representation of women and men on committees). In the case of Churches like my own that are still unwilling to allow women to be ordained, the best way forward in the short term may be to make a very clear distinction between the issue of ordination for women and the issue of women sharing in decision-making power—and to move forward strongly on the latter issue. This means that decision-making power on major issues of Church policy must no longer be reserved to those who are ordained. The reality is that women already play leading roles in the work of the Church—much more so than in other areas of public life. Surely, then, they are entitled to full representation on all policy-making bodies? Even those who are opposed to the ordination of women can scarcely defend any other position. And when women have taken their rightful place in decision-making in the Church, the world will have before it a living witness of how rich life can be when women and men work together in full mutual respect. Furthermore, Church people may then be willing to take a fresh look at the issue of ordination of women.

Oppression and Liberation: Church leaders and local Churches in various parts of the world have already demonstrated what a remarkable contribution they can make once they commit themselves to promoting integral human liberation. Among the outstanding names that spring to mind are Desmond Tutu, Allen Boesak, and Denis Hurley in South Africa; and the contribution of these Church leaders is matched by that of activist theologians such as Frank Chicane, Smangalisu Mkatshwa, Beyers Naudé and Albert Nolan. Those who are familiar with the South African scene will know that behind these very public figures stand a whole body of less well-known but equally dedicated and effective Church workers—many of them women—who have turned the Churches into powerful instruments of liberation and hope.

In Latin America one thinks at once of Church leaders like Helder Camera, Oscar Romero, Paulo Evaristo Arns, and Aloísio Lorscheider. Once again the theologians play an equally or even more significant role—people like Gustavo Gutiérrez, Jon Sobrino, Maria Clara Bingemer and Elsa Tamez. Theologians in South Africa, Latin America, the Philippines, Sri Lanka, Korea and other parts of the Third World (together with some exceptional First World theologians like Dorothee Sölle and Daniel Berrigan) have shown very clearly that theology can play a major role in the struggle for human liberation. It can provide a justification for that struggle. It does this, however, not by providing a mere ideological defence, a theory which seeks to give legitimacy to the struggle, but rather by putting people in touch with the authentic message of the Scriptures—and the challenge and hope which it brings. This is brought out very clearly in one of the most prophetic theological statements of recent times—a document entitled *The Road to Damascus: Cairos and Conversion*, issued by Third World Christians from seven nations. Their document 'rescues' God and Jesus from the distortions of a dualistic, other-worldly theology which presented God 'in the image and likeness of European kings, emperors and conquerors'.[6]

Racism: The major Churches have a fairly good record on this issue in recent times. Church leaders of widely different racial backgrounds work well together; and a solid effort has been made to internationalise the bureaucracies of both the WCC and the Roman Catholic Church. But the Churches must go further than this in promoting respect for the diversity of cultures. They must ensure that 'white' Western traditions, values, laws, attitudes and styles of action, are not imposed on people of other races and cultures as though they were of universal application. In this regard the Churches still have a long way to go. For, despite their multi-cultural and multi-racial composition, the major international Churches are structured and organised in a very traditional European manner with little influence from other cultures.

Population Explosion: It has to be pointed out that there are notable differences of approach between different Churches on

121

this issue. However, the divergence should not be exaggerated, since there is agreement on the need for responsible parenthood and for the avoidance of uncontrolled population growth. There is also agreement on the need to respect the fundamental freedom of would-be parents. The differences between the Churches (and within the Churches too) concern the *means* to be used to achieve and reconcile these ends, particularly in regard to the use of certain forms of artificial birth control. It is unfortunate that so much of the energy of many committed Christians is focused on the more controversial aspects of birth control, to the neglect of the underlying problem of poverty.

It would be a major contribution to the problem of over-population if Church leaders and theologians were to work out a commonly agreed and realistic moral teaching about the use of different forms of birth control. The absence of such agreement is a cause of serious scandal. The other big contribution that Church leaders can make is to emphasise the wider context of poverty within which the issue of the population explosion arises.

Refugees: The contribution of the Church has to be made at two distinct levels. The long-term solution to the problem of refugees lies, of course, in the overcoming of the twin causes of the problem—war and poverty. At the more immediate level, committed Christians and specialised Christian agencies can and do devote themselves to the very demanding task of helping displaced people. They need the continuing support of Church leaders and the Christian community at large. Where they need help perhaps most of all is in their efforts to ensure that refugees are not left for long in a state of dependency. The best help that can be given to those who have been displaced is to enable them to take responsibility for their own lives. In some cases this requires their resettlement in other countries; and Church leaders could play a more active role in promoting such resettlement. In other situations the best approach is to give support to those programmes—many of them pioneered by Church workers—which help displaced people to develop economic self-reliance and enable them to have a more active 'say' in political decisions which affect them.

Violence, Disarmament and Human Rights: I have linked these three issues together because I think the most important contribution the Church can make on them is to insist on the biblical notion of *shalom*, where peace is based on justice. For too long the major Churches were willing to settle for a kind of peace which was merely the preservation of a structurally unjust situation. When Church leaders led a struggle for human rights it was frequently only the rights of Christians and of the institutional Church that they had in mind. With the advent of various forms of liberation theology Churches have begun more and more to commit themselves in principle to the struggle for the fundamental rights of all; in practice, of course, there is still a certain selectivity and a tendency to put more emphasis on certain rights or the rights of certain groups.

Liberation theology encourages people to struggle for their fundamental human rights. In the media this is often presented as a theology of violence. In fact, however, it is, at its best, just the opposite. The Latin American liberation theologians have, for the most part, come out of a movement which confronts violent and oppressive force with non-violent resistance. More recently, the Churches played a prominent role in the peaceful movements that brought about radical change in Poland and East Germany. These movements were inspired by a radical Christian vision of a new society where human rights are respected and order in society is freely accepted rather than imposed by force. This ideal is, of course, shared by many people who are not Christians. But the inspiration of the life, death, and resurrection of Jesus provides believers with a very powerful motivation for dedicating themselves selflessly to a non-violent struggle for justice and human rights. And the social teaching of the Churches, as it has developed in recent years, provides Christians with an integral vision which clearly establishes the links between working to promote justice, working for peace and disarmament, and working to promote respect for the Earth on which we live.

Ecology: The Churches can make a major contribution on this issue by developing, preaching and practising a holistic spirituality which promotes partnership with nature rather than exploitation of its resources. This involves a notable change of

123

perspective in Christian teaching. It means abandoning the other-worldly, escapist spirituality which was common until fairly recently. But it also means rejecting the activist, human-centred spirituality which emerged more recently as a replacement for that old-style outlook. What we need is a spirituality which finds deep roots in the Earth as the gift of God, a gift to be treated with respect and care.[7]

In our efforts to develop such a spirituality we can learn much from the Amish people who have had the experience of living an alternative life-style for the past 250 years.[8] The Amish comprise ninety thousand people who live in a hundred rural settlements in twenty states of the USA. They have resisted the temptation to adopt the modern ecological destructive style of agriculture. They use machines sparingly, choosing those that do not make wasteful use of non-renewable sources of energy. And to ensure a good yield from their crops they rely mainly on crop rotation rather than pesticides and artificial fertilisers. Their ecologically sensitive life-style is based on a religious vision. In fact it is a Christian vision—though its emphasis and tone is radically different from the Christian spirituality which developed in Western society in recent centuries. Until recently the Amish were largely dismissed as old-fashioned but harmless cranks. But, with the emergence among Christians of a renewed understanding of the importance of partnership with nature, their achievement may be appreciated and their experience of living an alternative life-style and spirituality may prove invaluable to the major Christian Churches.

Unemployment: The Churches are not in a good position to overcome the problem of major long-term unemployment. Yet within the Churches there are communities of committed Christians that have shown some elements of a way forward. Various religious congregations and societies have succeeded in sharing out among their members the available resources and the work that has to be done. This means that they have, in effect, developed a way of eliminating unemployment within their own communities. Almost all their members have the opportunity to engage in worthwhile and fulfilling work.

The question arises, however, why this is seldom seen as relevant to the issue of unemployment in the wider society. It would

124

appear that the life of religious communities is commonly seen as quite different from, and unrelated to, the lives and problems of 'ordinary' people. Unfortunately, there are good grounds for this assumption. For, even today, many members of religious congregations live comfortable and protected lives. No wonder, then, that it does not occur to 'ordinary Christians' that they might find in such communities a possible approach towards dealing with unemployment! However, the major changes taking place at present in the life-style of many religious congregations is bringing them closer to the reality of daily life as lived in the outside world. Perhaps one result may be that society will find it has something to learn from the work-sharing approach adopted in religious communities.

It's not Enough

Anybody who reads through the above outline of what the Church can do towards resolving the various social justice problems must be struck by the feeling, 'it is not enough!'. There seems to be a great disparity between the size of the problems and the little the Churches can do. So long as we remain within the present framework or structures of society the Churches will remain confined to the fairly minor (though still significant) role of trying to alleviate some of the worst effects of the system.

I was tempted to omit the past few pages because the 'solutions' proposed in them seem so inadequate. But I included this material precisely to bring out the point that there is so little that can be done within the system. The conclusion which emerges clearly is that a commitment by the Churches to work for justice implies a commitment to a radical transformation of our present society. Once we opt for justice we no longer have the option of staying within the system. The problems are so profound and intractable that the only effective way to work for justice, peace and the integrity of creation is to search for an alternative model for human development. In the next chapter I shall go on to examine the contribution the Church can make to this search for alternatives.

6

The Church and the Search for Alternatives

I ENDED the previous chapter by pointing out that so long as we remain within the present structures of society the Churches will be limited to trying to lessen the bad results of the system. That was an acceptable role while the prevailing spirituality was one that saw the world as 'a valley of tears' through which we had to pass to come to our true home in the next life. But Christians today have come to see that such an escapist outlook is not truly Christian. It is being replaced by a spirituality which calls us to share in Christ's work of saving the world. In that perspective the role of the Church is no longer the same. It cannot be content to play the part of a nurse looking after the casualties of the system. It must play an active part both in challenging the present unjust structures and in pioneering alternatives. In particular it must help people to explore and develop models of human development which are more sustainable, more respectful of the Earth, more just and more humane than the present approach to development. For it is the present style of development which lies at the heart of most of the problems of social justice in our world today.

But is there any realistic alternative to the model of development which is already dominant in the Western world and is now being installed in the countries of what used to be called 'the Eastern bloc', as well as in most Third World countries? The answer is, yes. We have available to us at least the general outlines for an alternative model of development which would provide a fulfilled and human life for all the people of our planet. I have in mind the kind of approach proposed in 1989 in 'The Manila Declaration on People's Participation and Sustainable Development'. This declaration speaks of a people-centred, community-led 'process of economic, political and social change

126

that need not necessarily involve growth', the goal of which is 'the re-creation of society from the bottom up on a foundation of productive, sustainable communities'.[1] The 'Green Parties' in several countries—above all in West Germany—have translated this approach into practical policies.[2]

It is important to note that any realistic alternative model of development has to address not only the economic issues of production, consumption, appropriate technology and respect for the environment, but also the *political* issue of the decentralisation of power and the more effective participation by ordinary people in decision-making. I have written elsewhere about the promotion of a more participatory style of decision-making.[3] Here I shall concentrate mainly on the economic aspects of an alternative model of development.

Our Earth has enough productive land, as well as enough energy, minerals and other basic resources to ensure that everybody in the world is reasonably well fed and has the necessities for a fully human life—provided these resources are shared equitably and no nation or group is too greedy. But unfortunately the better-off and more powerful groups in our world are unwilling to agree to an equitable share-out of the Earth's resources. For that would mean that they would have to relinquish some of the unduly large share of 'the cake' which they now possess or control. This reluctance is not just due to greed. *The real problem lies in the ideological roots of the present model of economic development.* This is a rather sweeping statement which is also quite cryptic; so it requires further elucidation.

Ideology of Development

Development polices as presently adopted by governments all over the world are built around the notion of ever-increasing 'growth'. This means the production of more and more goods. But it also involves the using up of more and more resources of the Earth—the sources of energy, and the reserves of minerals, timber, clean water, etc. People everywhere have been led to expect that 'development' will increase the amount of goods available to them, and that there is no foreseeable limit to this kind of growth. The majority of the people in Western countries and a small but powerful minority in Eastern Europe and in 'the South' (the Third World) have experienced the benefits of this

127

'development' and they take for granted that it will continue. Furthermore, they assume that it can be extended to those who have not so far shared in the fruits of 'development'. Consequently, they see no reason why they should be asked to give up any of the fruits of past or future development.

So powerful is this ideological basis of development that those who are better off generally turn a blind eye to the fact that while they are growing richer others are growing poorer. More accurately, they are blind to the *connection* between their own growing wealth and the growing poverty of others. They do not advert to the fact that most of the available resources are going to a minority of the Earth's population. They assume that the poverty of the minority in 'the North' and of the majority in 'the South' is due to the fact that 'development' has not yet reached the poor, because of laziness, mismanagement, corruption, or misfortune—or simply because their turn has not yet come to be uplifted by the process of development which is assumed to be spreading out inevitably from the 'advanced' countries.

Faced with the ever-growing expectations of people—especially of powerful groups—many governments have compounded the problem by borrowing on an enormous scale; they assumed that the future growth of their economies would make it easy to pay off these debts at a later time. This left most Third World countries, as well as the United States and Ireland, burdened by massive debts which make it far more difficult in the long run to meet the expectations of the people. Furthermore, the style of 'development' adopted in most countries has involved a rapid 'cashing in' of ecological assets such as clean air, fresh water, natural forests, and reserves of oil or mineral resources. This too is a short-term approach creating greater problems in the long term.

The problem was made much more severe by the uncritical adoption of a policy of automation. This kind of short-term 'efficiency' allowed the powerful and vocal groups who had capital or secure jobs to get large increases in their income. But the price paid was to put many people out of work and give rise to large-scale permanent unemployment—'structural unemployment' as it is now called. This policy was justified as an inevitable and necessary part of the good thing called 'development'

How can the Church respond to this situation? Well, first of all, committed Church people can help the community at large to see through the myth of 'development'. Secondly, and above all, the Christian faith can provide hope to those who struggle to believe that some more viable alternative is possible. Thirdly, the Christian community and the institutional Church can give concrete help to those who face the daunting task of going against the prevailing certainties of our world by beginning to implement the elements of such alternatives.

What is The Economy'?

A key aim of Church-sponsored adult education programmes should be to rescue ordinary people from the misguided and even mythical notion of development which I have outlined. If people are to understand what *real* human development is about they must learn some basic facts about economics. For economic activity is such an important component of human development that we cannot afford to leave it to the economists! The unfortunate fact is that the majority of the students and professors of economics are, for the most part, dealing with only one part of economic activity. They concentrate very much on what is called the formal economy, which is concerned with such things as government revenue and spending, employment in the public and private sector, and the role of banks, trade unions, etc.

Some years ago the economists woke up to the fact that alongside this formal economy there is what has come to be called the *informal* economy. This term refers to a myriad of small-scale economic activities, which generally escape government supervision and taxation, e.g. a private agreement which a home owner may make with a local unemployed person to care for the garden or to mend a leaking roof; or a private arrangement to provide day-care for children. In many of the poorer countries of the world this informal economy is much more significant than the formal economy—even though it is largely ignored in the official statistics. Because the informal economy is more or less invisible to government planners, the official development plans tend to overlook it. (But when it becomes clear that there is no hope of creating enough jobs in the formal economy the planners say that the informal sector will make up the shortfall!)

Until very recently there was a widespread assumption that, taken together, the formal and the informal economy make up the total economy of any country. But this is a serious mistake,

129

for together they only constitute the *exchange* economy, where various goods and services are exchanged on some kind of commercial basis. Over and above this commercial economy there is a whole range of genuine economic activities which are not based on exchange at all. For instance, a married couple with skills but no 'job' may devote their time to building a house for themselves or for friends. Technically they are still 'unemployed'; but the house they build has the same economic value as one built by 'employed' people. Similarly, many people *freely* spend time counselling others, nursing sick or old people, caring for children, growing vegetables, or building up a community. None of these activities form part of the formal economy or even of the informal economy; they are not part of the *exchange* economy at all (though they would be, if they had been paid for in cash or in kind). Nevertheless, such activities may be just as important from an economic point of view as activities whose value is measured in money or some other form of exchange. Perhaps the most appropriate of the names that have been used to describe this kind of non-exchange economy is 'the economy of solidarity'.[4]

The whole object of this account of the economy is to provide a background to what I wish to say about the search for alternative models of development. The crucial point is that alternative development will have to do much more with 'the economy of solidarity' than with the exchange economy. I stress this in order to forestall at least some of the objections that are commonly put forward to the kind of proposals I wish to make. Most of the objections come from economists whose mindset is such that they are inclined to equate economic activity with the *exchange* economy, and even, to a large extent, with the *formal* sector of the exchange economy. Consequently, when they say that proposals about alternative styles of agriculture or about work-sharing are 'unrealistic', they themselves are not being fully realistic. They are not taking account of, or not giving full weight to, 'the economy of solidarity'.

One reason why most economists overlook or undervalue 'the economy of solidarity' is that they want economics to become more scientific, which, for them, means that it will concentrate on what can be measured exactly. But it is far more difficult to measure and compare the values that people use when they are working on a non-commercial basis. Some of such work is enormously valuable from an economic point of view; people undertake it, however, not because they will get money or goods in exchange but simply because they feel obliged or inspired to do so by their traditions or by social pressure or by their personal moral or religious convictions. At this point there is no possibility of developing an abstract universal science of economics which is independent of such things as culture and religion. In the economy of solidarity, economics is inextricable from culture, from morality, from religion.

The conclusion from all this is that the search for an alternative model of development is not a purely economic one, if economics is understood in the traditional sense. It has as much to do with religion as with economics; it is as much a matter of personal morality and of communal culture as it is of politics. Therefore Church leaders cannot be content to encourage Christians to engage in this search in much the same way as they might encourage people to become good scientists or good artists. The matter is much closer than that to the heart of the Christian faith.

The official Church and its leaders believe they have an important contribution to make on the subject of what it means to live an authentically human life. But the only way in which people today can live truly human lives is to find a better understanding than we have at present of what is meant by human development. For this reason the Church and its leaders must concern themselves in a very committed and active way with the search for alternatives. They must see this as a matter of the incarnation of the Christian faith into people's daily lives and into human cultures. This is of the very highest priority for the Church and its leaders because it is at the heart of evangelisation, of bringing the good news to the world of today.

Ecological Alternatives

In the search for an alternative style of human development a good place to begin is with the pressing need for a more ecologically sensitive type of development. If we treat our environment only as a resource to be *exploited* we are likely before long to kill the goose that lays the golden eggs..We have to learn to live more effectively in partnership with Nature, respecting it and

131

caring for it, so that we can have authentic development. I have already written about this in general terms in chapter 1 above and in a previous book.[5] But that is not enough. Three further steps are necessary:

—Firstly, there is need for careful analysis of the various values that one is looking for in adopting an alternative style of development; we must be clear about how these differ from the dominant values of the present approach. A good deal of work has already been done on this topic and it is available in a fairly accessible form in such sources as the *IFDA Dossier* which is published six times each year by the International Foundation for Development Alternatives.[6] Another interesting example of this kind of work is the account given by Richard Cartwright Austin of three interdependent values that are involved in agriculture. These are *sustenance* (which includes not only food for the farmer but also the joy of work and the reward of beauty), *conservation* (which involves care for the health of the land) and *production* (which means growing food for sale to others). The problem with modern agriculture is that it concentrates so much on production that it neglects the values of sustenance and conservation.[7] Most of those who engage in alternative agriculture are people who have deliberately 'dropped out' (to a considerable extent) from the formal economy. They are committed to promoting the kind of values that are important in 'the economy of solidarity'. So they are interested not just in a more ecological type of farming but also in a whole style of human development that challenges the prevailing model. They are seeking a more wholesome and fulfilling life-style within a fairly self-sufficient local community. And they would want this community to be equitable, participative and largely self-governing, to rely mainly on renewable materials and energy sources and to help all of its members to discover and develop their various gifts and talents.

—A second step that is needed is to work out ways in which there can be a gradual (but not too gradual!) transition to an alternative style of development. Once again the *IFDA Dossier* is a useful source. And once again Richard Cartwright Austin makes a useful contribution—this time by sketching out a possible scenario for the transition at the local level to an ecologically respectful and humanly fulfilling model of farming.[8]

132

—The third step is the practical one of 'taking the plunge'. There are already many individuals, groups and families who have committed themselves to putting such beliefs into practice. We need to know more about what they are doing, and to get to know some of them personally. They need our encouragement and support; and they need some of us to join them. The world needs far more of such people, for they are its future.

Transitional Measures

At present most people would find it very difficult to make the radical break involved in opting out of the mainstream economy and moving into an alternative type of economy. But this does not mean that those of us who are not able or willing to make the break at this time have to just wait until the situation changes. There are a whole series of fairly minor changes which have a real value here and now and which can at the same time open up further possibilities in the future. They can ease the way into a situation where large numbers of people will be able to move into the alternative economy. The following are some of these transitional changes for which we can campaign, in order to bridge the gap between the present and the future we hope for:

—Just as governments in several countries have given a preferential rate of taxation to lead-free fuel for motor cars so they could eliminate or reduce sales tax on organically grown food. This can be justified for ecological reasons as well as on the grounds that it will help to promote the health of the consumers and will provide more employment. Similar concessions could be made for hand-crafted goods.

—At present most governments are investing enormous sums of money in the building of new roads. They can be pressured into switching much of this money into the development of railways rather than roads and providing a really effective and ecologically sensitive public transport system. This will make it possible for people who at present really need a motor car to choose to live without one.

—Authorities everywhere can be pressured into reserving certain traffic lanes for public service vehicles and car-pool vehicles. In this way there will be a further incentive to rely on public or shared transport.

133

—Special tracks can be provided for bicycles as an incentive to commuters to use this form of transport.

—Various tax incentives can be offered to those who choose to work on small family farms; what is in question here is a reversal of present policies which favour large-scale factory farming.

—At present most governments invest a great deal of the tax-payers' money in ensuring that the State has adequate supplies of energy; the State's involvement comes both in the form of direct investment and in various concessions made to companies which provide energy. A good deal of this investment ought to be re-directed to small-scale energy producers, e.g. people who set up viable means of tapping the energy of sunlight or wind or water.

—In general a great deal of the very significant financial incentives offered at present to big business ought to be direct-ed instead to small-scale, ecologically sensitive, labour-saving enterprises.

Changes of this kind are all within the bounds of what is politically possible at present, provided a significant number of people campaign for them. Success on such issues could lead on to a campaign for a more radical step. This further step is that any community of people who opt to set up an alternative ecologically-sensitive economy should have the right to nego-tiate with the government about opting out of certain parts of the overall 'umbrella' provided by the modern State.

I am thinking here of the enormous amounts of tax-payer's money used to support the machinery of the State and the bureaucracy which is designed to support the present economy and the social system built upon it. Those who opt for an alter-native economy ought to be able to choose to provide at least some of their own alternative services instead; and if they do so they ought to be relieved of a notable part of the burden of taxation. For such an approach to become viable there would have to be significant numbers of people willing to opt out of the present system and set up alternative communities with a high degree of political awareness. These communities would have to be large enough to provide the kind of alternative services that could replace much of the present fabric of government. This may seem unrealistic at present, but it could become a real option within a few years if a momentum for radical change is generated by committed people working in a determined but not fanatical way for the easier changes which I outlined above.

Partnership and work-sharing[9]

In the previous pages I have been writing about the need to move to a more ecologically sensitive type of farming. Another starting-point for an exploration of alternative development is the very practical issue of unemployment. Meaningful work is a necessary (but not sufficient) condition for human fulfilment. In the world today the advance of technology has shifted the main burden of work from human labour to machines; but in doing so it has left millions of people jobless. The best remedy for unemployment is not the abolition of all modern technology but the adoption of work-sharing practices of various kinds.

In fact the people in many of the 'less developed' parts of the world (including the West of Ireland where I come from) have practised different kinds of work-sharing over the years. Trades and professions are much less specialised and exclusive than they are in the modern urban situation. This means that different kinds of work are shared quite widely, according to the needs of the situation and the talents and interests of the workers. People who live on very small family farms supplement their income by working as part-time building-workers, dress-makers, painters, cooks, and so on. But the present model of economic development treats such part-time work as marginal and puts these workers at a disadvantage in various ways. What is needed is a fairly thorough shift of emphasis and priorities which would offer incentives for the kind of work-sharing that would allow everybody to have enough work to earn an adequate living, rather than restricting work to a relatively small number of specialists.

This means that those who have jobs at present would give up over-time and even part of their regular work-hours (perhaps one or two days a week), in order to provide work for those who are unemployed. Thus job insecurity would be eliminated or greatly lessened, since there would be more jobs all round. Everybody would have access to a significant amount of income-earning work, and everybody would have time for other creative and fulfilling occupations. In some cases these other commit-ments might bring in some extra income. In other cases they

135

would be rewarding in non-monetary ways. I am thinking of the satisfaction which many people get from renovating their homes, or from growing their own vegetables or from serving the community in different ways. It must be added, however, that there would be need for a fairly widespread and creative programme of adult education to enable people to discover their gifts and talents, and to enable them to develop their interests. Without such an education many people would become bored and perhaps destructive.

The price to be paid for work-sharing on this scale would be a reduction in the standard of living of many workers. However, this reduction would not be as great as one might expect at first sight; for the working community would no longer have the burden of paying heavy taxes to provide unemployment benefits for the jobless.

I am not suggesting that work-sharing is a magic formula that will solve all the problems arising from the present style of development. The truth is that economics is such an inexact science that nobody can really come up with an effective way to guarantee full employment; and some attempts to 'make' jobs can create worse problems in the long run. But work-sharing offers notable short-term and long-term advantages. In the short-term it can help us to break out of the disastrous economic and psychological problems that arise when up to half of the work force in many countries is unemployed or underemployed. Over a longer period of time it should bridge the gulf that has grown up between over-burdened workers on the one hand and the alienated unemployed on the other. In this way it would help to create a climate where all the members of the community can together take responsibility for the welfare of all. I must add, however, that if work-sharing is to be effective it will have to be combined with radical changes in life-style—and this is the next point to which I turn.

Alternatives in Life-style

There is an urgent need for some notable changes in life-style to complement the changes in economic policy outlined above. We will have to become less wasteful and somewhat more puritan in our mode of living. Cheap and efficient public and semi-public transport could replace much of the private motoring.

136

Walking and cycling could make a come-back. We would have less of the 'throw-away' culture—for instance, clothes would be designed to last longer; and we would have to abandon the consumer-culture in which last year's fashions in clothes are no longer acceptable. Consumption of candy and soft drinks would be greatly reduced. With less money to spend on luxuries, people would have to change their preferred patterns of recreation. Community activities in the neighbourhood centre might largely replace the 'night out' in the local bar and other more wasteful forms of recreation.

Of course, this may seem unrealistic. Yet there is plenty of evidence to show that people are willing to exchange affluence and consumer goods for creative and meaningful activity. The most obvious example is the fact that when young people get married and begin to rear a family they commonly make just the kind of changes I have listed above—and they are happy to do so because they have found a more meaningful goal in life. Furthermore, a lot of people are now giving up highly-paid jobs to return to a much less luxurious rural style of life, simply in order to benefit from the values that cannot be bought—the sense of being part of a community, the beauty of nature, and the peace that comes from living close to the Earth. I should add that it seems likely that when the ecological crisis really begins to bite in some years' time, all of us will find that we have to put up with much greater restrictions. Thus changes of the kind I am suggesting are by no means *objectively* unrealistic. It is just that it seems *politically* unthinkable that people be asked to undertake them voluntarily at this time.

Nevertheless, proposals about large-scale work-sharing are dismissed as unrealistic by those who hold power in society. The idea of asking workers as a whole to make such sacrifices does not even get on the agenda of the negotiations between 'the social partners' (i.e. employers, workers, and government). Perhaps one reason for this is that the employers, the trade unions and the government do not make room at the negotiating table for the other social partners—the long-term unemployed and those who have been forced to emigrate in search of work.

Whatever the reason, the fact is that a change of policy and approach which is quite realistic in principle is in practice seen as a non-starter. We remain paralysed through an absence of the kind of imaginative planning that would be needed to work out a credible alternative. Behind this failure of imagination and of realistic planning lies a lack of vision. We are not sufficiently concerned for the welfare of the community and of humankind as a whole—or if we have such concern we fail to relate it to the reality of political life.

Inspiration from the Bible

The task of building alternatives is so daunting that it seems almost hopeless. In seeking a way forward we can, perhaps, find inspiration in the approach of the liberation theologians of Latin America. They look realistically at the situation of oppression in which their people find themselves, and they find little basis for hope. But where human hope fails they turn to the Bible and find in the story of Moses and his people a hope that lies beyond human expectation.

The person who wishes to find hope that an alternative model of human development is possible can also look at the Bible. Perhaps the most apt parallel is the story of the return from exile of the people of God. Just as the Israelite people were carried off into exile so we, the people of the world today, find ourselves in a state of exile. We are no longer at home on the Earth, for we are no longer living in partnership with each other and with Nature. We are alienated, lonely, unrooted, lost.

The Jewish exile lasted for seventy years. Then, when all human hope should have been dead, there came the return. Not an earth-shaking event but just a minor emigration of a determined few (Ezra ch.8). The return of this remnant was experienced as the gift of God. But this gift did not come in military glory; it was rather the result of patient planning, negotiation and diplomacy (Nehemiah 2:3-6). Having returned, the former exiles struggled to revive their culture, encapsulated in their Law (Nehemiah 8:1—10:38). With great determination they set about rebuilding their city and their Temple (Nehemiah 3:1—4:23). But they were no saints; not long after the return the strong were once again taking advantage of the weak (Nehemiah 5:1-6).

Despite all its inadequacies, this return was a rebirth for God's people, a new beginning. World history has been radically changed because of this apparently minor event. For the Israelites—and for us Christians—the history of that time has

138

become a vivid reminder that God can draw new life out of utter failure. There is hope even for people that, by human reckoning, have lost all hope. Two thousand five hundred years ago it seemed that the history of the Jewish people had effectively come to an end. But out of the exile they came back—politically weak, economically impoverished, but enriched in spirit. They had been forged into a people who were able to endure and survive and cling to their own traditions. They had learned much from the religion and the gods of their neighbours—but they had a renewed determination to be faithful to the God who was faithful to them when all human hope had failed.

The Jewish experience of exile and return moulded them into a people that was able to endure centuries and millennia of persecution, and could still look forward to a future as a free people in their own land. Their return gives *us* hope: hope that the people of the world as a whole may also return from exile; hope that we too, by God's grace and our own efforts, may live in dignity on an Earth where we can be both free and at home.

Prodigal People

The Bible also contains another exile story. It is the more personal tale of the Prodigal Son, the young man who squandered his wealth and only came to his senses when he found himself helpless and hopeless in exile. The situation of the better-off people of the world today has much in common with his experience. Like him we have squandered what we inherited and can be held responsible for our situation of exile. Like him we have the possibility of coming to our senses and coming back home with the intention of living a more frugal life in future. And like him we may find that the return is far easier than we would have expected. Once we repent of our profligate ways, our partners in creation, and the Earth itself, will warmly welcome us home and offer us a fuller and more comfortable life than we deserve.

The story of the return of the Prodigal reminds us that our return from our exile situation cannot be just a purely political and economic happening. It will have to involve an element of personal conversion: sorrow for our wasteful luxury of the past, a willingness to change our ways, a determination to live frugally in future—and an openness to accept the surprising and prodigal generosity of Mother Earth, our home.

139

A Source for Hope?

These exile stories are inspiring; but they may not be quite enough for us. Perhaps they are not sufficient to break the hopelessness and sense of paralysis that seems a central part of our exile experience. We may need some stronger evidence to convince us that a return is possible. For me, a return from exile would begin with knowing that the suffering and destruction of the past can somehow bear fruit in new life. I need to know that the destruction of the rain forests is not irreversible. I need an indication that the spiral of poverty and population explosion in the poorer countries can somehow be halted. I look at the centuries of exploitation of 'the South'—the slave trade, the elimination of vibrant cultures, the clever replacement of a cruel colonial system by an equally destructive and cruel neo-colonial system—and I have to be convinced that this is not the end of the story. I have to be convinced that, somehow, the long exile of the people of the world can be the prelude to a new world, richer and better than that of the past. By some miracle I must be able to experience the *loss* as a *gain*. The only way I can hope for such a miracle is by exploring the mystery of the Cross.

At the heart of the Christian faith lies the cross. It recalls for us a historical event—the execution of Jesus. It represents a doctrine of our faith, an article of the Creed. But it has become something more: it is the fundamental symbol which bridges the gap between faith and the tragedies of daily life. Every day people die holding a crucifix, people face up to impossible situations strengthened by prayer before the crucifix, and people who have suffered apparently irreparable hurt and loss are able to be reconciled by experiencing solidarity with Christ on the cross.

Literally, the cross is an instrument of torture and death, a gallows or gibbet which has just one purpose—to bring a criminal to a slow, painful, and shameful death deprived of all dignity. Yet when committed Christians take up a crucifix they do not feel a thrill of horror and fear as they would if somebody gave them, say, a picture of a person tortured in Guatemala. On the cross we see an image of a tortured man, but we don't regret his torture and death. We can even be *glad* that this awful thing has happened. The power of Christ's death is such that it has transformed the cross from being an image of shame to an image of nobility and glory. It evokes in us not horror and grief but gratitude and love. And yet the suffering and shame are not absent. They remain real historical facts that are not denied or played down by the symbol of the cross. But they have become suffused with love and joy.

The cross represents the rejection of Christ, the failure of his mission. Yet our faith now reveals to us, as it did to the disciples at Emmaus, that for Jesus 'it was necessary to suffer these things' (Lk 24:26). By faith we learn to set this failure in a wider context—'beginning with the books of Moses and the writings of all the prophets' (Lk 24:27) and culminating in the resurrection of Jesus to new life and his sharing of that life with all who believe in him. In that full context we can now experience Christ's death as part of a pattern; we see it as central to God's loving plan. The shameful death of Jesus is meaningful and even infinitely worthwhile when it is seen as the focal point in the providential history of God's people.

Our faith in the cross of Jesus must be allowed to throw light on every aspect of our lives. It cannot be confined to some narrowly defined 'religious' sphere, or to the private aspects of life. It must permeate out political beliefs, enabling us to believe that a situation that seems hopeless can be transformed. We must apply it to the desperate situation of the world today, allowing it to convince us that just as the death of Jesus was not the end but the beginning of a new life, so there can be a return for the peoples of the Earth from our exile experience. The exiles who walked back from Babylon to begin a new life in their own land had to face hardship and insecurity. And their leaders had a hard task in persuading the powers of the time to allow the exiles to undertake this project of restoration. But what was hardest of all for the people and their leaders was to have *faith*—to believe that the venture was *possible*. It is the same with us today. Insecurity and some hardship is the lot of those who are trying to build an alternative society based on partnership between people and partnership with the Earth. And it is no easy task to persuade governments and international agencies to take such projects seriously and to give them the support they need. But what is most difficult of all for those who are involved is to have *faith*— to believe that the received wisdom of the mainline economists and the politicians is not the final word on our world, to believe that an alternative model of human development is possible and that it can be realised.

141

The change from 'exile' to 'return' in our world today is politically so unlikely that it calls for an evident exercise of God's power. In other words, it requires a kind of miracle. But this is a miracle that God cannot do alone, since it requires people like us as instruments of divine power. It is never easy to believe in a miracle; and it is particularly difficult when we ourselves are called to be the instruments that will bring it about.

The miracle of return from exile of the Jewish people could only take place when a small believing remnant were prepared to put their faith into practice. Once they started their journey back, the miracle had already begun to take place. Can such miracles take place in today's world? There are indications that they can. I think of what the Chinese did forty years ago, when they showed that a war-torn and desperately poor nation could become self-sufficient within a few years. I think of what the Nicaraguans achieved in their struggle for genuine human development before they were swamped by the Contras and the economic pressure of powerful and hostile neighbours.

At present I think especially of what the Palestinian people are doing in their struggle to overcome oppression. They have come to realise that the economic and cultural aspects of the struggle for liberation are at least as important as the military and political aspects. The Palestinians are now making heroic sacrifices in an effort to develop some measure of economic self-sufficiency. In doing so they show that a people determined to take charge of their own destiny can do so in spite of all the odds. The transformation of the consciousness of the Palestinian people is so radical that it has been compared to the change that took place in the first Christians on the day of Pentecost.[10] And this change of a whole nation has been evoked and coordinated by a corps of dedicated leaders. They were the ones who believed that the miracle was possible; and by their faith they have made it possible for others.

It will have to be like this in the world as a whole and in each country. Some few have to believe that a 'return from exile' is possible. And then they have to begin to find ways in which that possibility can be brought into being. It is the kind of task that requires unlimited faith. And it is a challenge that lies at the heart of the Christian faith, for Christians are called to share in Christ's work of bringing salvation to the world.

The invention and implementation of alternatives to the present destructive and unjust model of development is a challenge for individual Christians and for small groups. But it is also a challenge which is the concern of the official Church. Not that the Church as an institution is called to become involved in establishing new political parties and new styles of economic activity. But Church leaders can give active inspiration, encouragement and support to those who are exploring alternatives. They can swing the full weight of the Church behind various pioneering efforts. Here, I mention just a few of the ways in which they could help:

—Church leaders could explain and promote among the wider Christian community the efforts of the groups who have set up alternative distribution networks for Third World products such as coffee, tea, and craftwork; these networks are designed to be an alternative to the present exploitative system which deprives the primary producers of a fair price for their products.[11]

—Church leaders could encourage the Christian community to become actively involved in consumer cooperatives, housing cooperatives, credit unions, production cooperatives, etc.

—The Church could become more involved in human relations training programmes with the aim of improving worker-employer relations and of helping workers become effectively involved in management.

—Perhaps most importantly of all, the official Church and its leaders could give active moral and practical support to individuals and groups who are pioneering a more human and sustainable approach to development—those who have adopted work-sharing practices of various kinds and those who have opted for ecologically sensitive styles of farming or of living.

Support from the official Church and its leaders in such ventures would help people believe that an alternative world is possible. In giving such support the Church would be carrying out a significant part of its work of evangelisation. For it would be passing on good news about God's will to save the world. And it would be helping people to respond in faith to this good news.

Theology for Whom?

IN THE PREVIOUS two chapters I have been looking at the role which the Church can play within *society* to make it more just, caring and ecologically respectful. In the following two chapters I want to focus attention on justice within *the Church itself*. For the words and actions of Christians in relation to the world will lack credibility if we do not face up to the ways in which there is a lack of justice in the structures and practices of the institutional Church. Injustice is essentially the misuse of power. Within the Church different individuals and groups exercise various kinds of power, e.g. control of finances or of appointments or the right to speak on behalf of the Church. But perhaps the most important power in the Church is the ability to articulate the Christian message and to explore its meaning for today's world. All Christians are called to exercise this power, but to do it effectively one needs to have some familiarity with theology. So it is important to look at theology as a power which can be used respectfully and shared with others or, on the other hand, can be used unjustly to control and dominate others.[1]

Section One: Theology as Power

There is a power that is liberating and a power that is dominating. The person who is doing theology is exercising one or other of these types of power; and frequently there is a bit of both. In this chapter I shall explore these two aspects of theology. The use of the word 'theology' in the title of the chapter might give some people the impression that I am dealing here with something abstract and theoretical. But in fact my aim is very practical. From a positive point of view I want to encourage people to engage more consciously in the kind of theology that helps to set people free. On the negative side I want to help people advert to what is going on when they are trying to dominate others by means of theology, or when others are trying to dominate them.

Theology as Liberating

In recent years we have become so aware of the dangers of power that we could forget that there is a power which is liberating. It is the power the first humans were given when they were invited to rule the earth and name the animals (Gen 1:28; 2:19–20). This invitation need not be interpreted solely or even mainly as a mandate to control the external world. Much more important is the challenge of putting a name on what is going on within us and giving meaning and shape to our own lives. Without that, any attempt we make to name and shape the world around us is unlikely to succeed.

I myself have spent about fifty years learning how to articulate my experience and to take responsibility for what I do with it; and I still have a long way to go. But I can look back on various key moments which have occurred in every sphere of my life. For instance, it was a breakthrough when I was first able to acknowledge and put a name on some of my more threatening feelings—fear, unhappiness or anger. I was also making progress when I could give words for the first time to some deep commitment which had grown within me, such as a commitment to personal integrity.

In this chapter I want to focus attention on the importance of giving expression to specifically religious experiences, attitudes, and values. Such articulation is what I understood theology to be. I begin with some personal examples.

—I remember the day I first recognised that doing theology was for me a life-giving experience. A fellow-student had just explained that there was no need for me to study Karl Rahner's book, *The Theology of Death* so intensely since it would scarcely count in our degree examination; and I found myself replying that I was studying it because it was exciting and enlightening— it gave words to an aspect of my own experience that craved expression.

—I remember the insecurity combined with a sense of freedom, of the day nearly twenty-five years ago when I walked down the street admitting to myself that the understanding of 'intrinsic evil' which I had always held might be wrong.

145

—I remember the light that dawned for me when I grasped Rahner's point that *all* of human history is 'salvation history' and that the explicit history of salvation recorded in the Bible could help me to interpret the wider history.

—I recall the excitement and challenge of reading Rosemary Haughton's early book, *On Trying To Be Human*; there she dared to translate the technical language of theology back into the everyday language of real-life experience—so that words like 'grace' and 'conversion' began to refer to events I could recognise in my own life.

—I remember a moment of insight during a workshop some years ago when it came home to me that ultimately my spirituality is not just the practical application of truths I believe; rather, it is prior to such truths and is their source, since it is what shapes and moves me.

—I cannot quite recall when it was that I first came to see the distinction between morality and religion; but I can think of many occasions after that light dawned for me when I felt enriched by that insight and sad that many other Christians still failed to make the distinction.

Choosing Life

Enlightenment and empowerment are two words that describe the effect on me of the theological insights I have mentioned, along with dozens of similar instances and hundreds of others that were more diffuse yet equally significant. I believe that without them I would be poorer, less human, less able to take responsibility for my own life. And without them I would also be less able to relate responsibly to other people whose lives intersect with my own.

I know people who have allowed the whole area of religion and theology to be fenced off or packed away, insulated from insight, growth, and increasing responsibility. Meanwhile, in almost all the other spheres of their lives they have had significant moments of breakthrough—in the area of human relationships, in their understanding of politics, or in the spheres of art or literature. The combination of stagnation in the religious area with growth in other areas has unfortunate effects. There is a marginalisation of their religious beliefs and values, simply because these are no longer in harmony with their other values

146

and attitudes. Some clash with religious authorities may easily provoke in any of these people an explicit rejection of Christian faith and belief in God. In cases like this the rejection is not experienced as a loss but as a liberation from a set of beliefs and values that no longer carry any real conviction.

One of the most important ways in which committed Christians can help people is by encouraging them to take their religious values and beliefs out of mothballs and integrate them into the part of their lives where they are actively living and growing. By doing this we are empowering people, helping them to exercise a power that is liberating. The most obvious way for me as a Christian minister and theologian to do this is to give expression, in my preaching, writing and conversation to the deeper hopes, fears and values of the individuals or communities with whom I am communicating. If I succeed in this I shall be bringing into the light parts of their experience that had been dormant or unrecognised. My reward will be to see faces light up as my words strike home. (At other times I may know I have succeeded if I see faces fall; for the enlightenment that comes may not always be a comfortable one.) What people choose to do with this articulation of their experience depends on themselves. They may act on it or allow it to slip out of consciousness again.

In Scripture I find many models for this kind of activity. There is the magnificent canticle where Miriam celebrates the liberation of her people from slavery (Ex 15:21). There is the Book of Lamentations which expresses the tragedy of the people of Israel. The Book of Numbers gives expression to the laws under which the Jews chose to live. The apocalyptic parts of the Bible articulate the deep religious hopes and fears of those who were called to speak God's word to this people. But it is important to note that those who composed the chants of victory, the lamentations, the laws, or the apocalyptic visions, were not speaking in a vacuum; their words could only be truly meaningful when they found an echo—or a target—in the hearts of those who heard them.

Doing Theology with People

I have said that the most obvious way for me to exercise a liberating theological power is to articulate for people their religious experience. But I believe that is only a second best.

147

There is a better way: instead of trying to speak *for* people I may help them to articulate their own religious experience *for themselves*. On occasion I have had the opportunity to facilitate a group in doing this. Usually, it is better not to give any name to such a process, lest we become too self-conscious or pompous. The purpose is to give a voice to those who have been (relatively) voiceless. When it goes well it is a life-giving and liberating experience for people as they struggle to articulate the deepest aspects of their own experience, to write their own personal histories and that of the community—and perhaps of a whole people.

Over the past fifteen years I have worked with various groups whose members have been attempting, in small but quite exciting ways, to articulate the deeper aspects of their experience. These people are really searching for a spirituality that meets the needs of their hearts. They often find that their task is to give expression to a spirituality that was already implicit in their hearts and lives. For the most part, those who are involved would not consider that they are doing theology. But a very small number see this work as a deliberate attempt to develop a more relevant theology, as a supplement and corrective to the 'received' theology. On one or two occasions we have ventured to call it 'participative theologising'. Some of this theological work takes place in movements, centres, or programmes that operate under Church auspices. But there are other situations where official or semi-official Church encouragement is lacking. In these circumstances it may take place in educational or development programmes that have little or no connection with any of the Churches.

There is a certain convergence between different strands of this emergent theology. An informal network is developing in different countries as key members from various groups come together to learn from each other or to engage in common training programmes or lobbying activities. All this gives me hope. Not the kind of hope that comes from counting numbers and calculating the effect of forces and trends. It is rather the hope of one who sees seed being scattered and believes that some of it may take root and bear fruit a hundredfold.

The Role of the Church Authorities

What I have been saying so far about theology is incomplete. I need to supplement it by putting more stress on the fact that

148

Christians do not do theology in isolation but as part of the Christian community. The reflection and articulation of which I am speaking ought to be stimulated and coordinated by the people who have been given authority in the Church. These authority people are of two kinds. There are those who have the authority of *office*—bishops and ministers of all kinds. And there are others whose authority comes from *competence, training, and specialisation*; these are the theologians.

The people who hold either kind of authority are called to serve the community by helping them to articulate their Christian experience and to interpret it in the light of the Judaeo-Christian tradition, a tradition embodied in a whole complexus of symbols, doctrines, stories, values, laws, institutions and roles. Within this tradition the Scriptures have been given a normative role; and the life and teaching of Jesus is the ultimate criterion in the interpretation of Scripture and of the wider tradition. The authorities have a particular responsibility to ensure that the tradition does not become fossilised and that it is not expressed in misleading or false ways. Of course the authorities themselves may fail in this, either by neglect or by allowing themselves to be 'bought' to serve the interests of some power group. Prophetic figures arise within the community to challenge the authorities, and by doing so to help them in their task.

Turnabout in Latin America

All this can be illustrated vividly from the history of the Church in the countries of Latin America. Over several hundred years the dominant theology, spirituality, and religious rites in these countries had become quite distorted. To a considerable extent they no longer reflected the life-experience of the mass of the people. The ordinary people undoubtedly experienced themselves as oppressed. But most of the clergy and theologians (to whom fell the task of articulating the experience of the people) had betrayed their people. In their teaching, preaching and ceremonies, they were in fact encouraging the people to interpret their suffering and oppression as the will of God.

Then, in the years immediately after Vatican II, a few prophetic figures succeeded in evoking a massive conversion on the part of very many of the authorities. From 1968 onwards in several (though not all) Latin American countries the majority

149

of the bishops and theologians began to play their proper role. They set out to correct the distortions of the past and to help the community to develop a new theology, a new spirituality and a revised set of religious ceremonies. The purpose was both to evoke and to express an authentic Christian response to the situation of oppression in which the great majority of the people lived.

One result of this conversion of Church leaders and theologians has been the emergence of a powerful theology and spirituality of liberation. This articulates the yearning of people for freedom. But it also helps people to find a way of struggling that still respects the values of non-violence and respect for others. Side by side with this there has developed a spirituality and a model of the Church centred on small communities mainly among the poor. These communities are experienced as places where oppressed people can maintain or regain something of their human dignity and their responsibility for others. The conversion of the Church authorities has also led to the emergence and training of very many gifted local leaders—men and women (and youths as well) who remain part of the poor communities in which they live, but who offer a respectful and effective religious ministry to their people.

When this change began to take place about twenty years ago the results were really dramatic. Quite suddenly the Church was no longer an ideological obstacle to the struggle for liberation. Instead it began to play a crucial role in the whole process of liberation. Consequently, the Church authorities in that situation did not have the problem of trying to find ways of being relevant to the daily lives of the community.

First World Issues

What a contrast there is between this Latin American situation and the state of the Church that prevails in Western countries. Here, we are confronted by issues that are perhaps just as crucial as those of the Third World:

1. We are aware—or half-aware—that the threat of nuclear and/or biological warfare hangs over the whole earth. At any moment our own lives and much of the life of the planet may be wiped out.

2. Even if war is avoided, nuclear accidents and the ongoing dumping of nuclear and chemical poisons threaten the survival of our world.

3. Almost everywhere, 'national security' is being invoked to prevent ordinary people from participating effectively in making the decisions that affect their lives.

4. Alongside all this, there is the continuing treatment of women as second-class people, within a patriarchal system.

5. Furthermore, the very model of exploitative 'development' which is causing impoverishment and oppression in the *Third* World is polarising our *First* World societies as well; it is creating a growing minority of poor and marginalised people who have little chance of sharing the fruits of 'development' and are increasingly resented by the better-off people as parasites on society.

6. In addition to this, in many parts of the world, groups divided from each other by race, culture, or religion are on the brink of genocidal conflict.

7. Meanwhile, ever increasing unemployment, the escalation of drug abuse, and the great increase in terrorism and violent crime all threaten the quality of human life.

These issues singly and collectively must be seen as 'religious' in so far as they have to do with the ultimate meaning and values of life. In fact it is doubtful if there has ever before been a time when society was presented with so many and such pressing religious questions at the same time. Yet, amazingly, most Church authorities (not only bishops, but also theologians) are moaning that Western society has become secularised, that it is no longer concerned with religious issues! Could it be that we are so trapped in the traditional articulation of religious issues that we are unable to appreciate the full religious significance of these new questions?

Inadequate Response

On most of these major issues the Church has not succeeded in articulating a spirituality that is found irrelevant and inspiring by large numbers of people. When I look at the seven issues which I have listed, it seems to me that the Church has made an important, but limited, contribution on just two of them—the last two (no. 6 and no. 7). So, before making any critical comments about the Church, let me first note its positive achievements on these two issues:

—In regard to the divisions between races and cultures: over the centuries Christians have developed a variety of models of

151

community life—especially for those who take religious vows; and most of these religious communities have been given the blessing and support of the official Church. Many of these congregations include people of different races and cultures, often living in harmony in the same community. In this way the Church has shown in practice that it is possible for communities of committed people to transcend racial and cultural barriers— and even that cultural and racial differences can, at best, bring a great enrichment to individuals and communities.

—As regards the threat to the quality of life from unemployment, drugs, etc: as I noted towards the end of chapter 5 above, various religious congregations and societies share out in a fair way among their members the available resources and the work that has to be done; in this respect they offer a kind of model for the elimination of gross disparities in life-style. They also offer some elements of a model for how unemployment might be eliminated, since almost every member of these communities has the opportunity to engage in worthwhile and fulfilling work. Furthermore, the more successful of the religious communities offer their members the kind of support-structures that make it less likely that those with difficulties will escape into drug abuse or alcoholism.

In regard to the other five issues I am afraid that the contribution of the Church—especially the Western Church—has been very limited indeed:

1. On the question of disarmament, Church authorities are seriously divided; instead of giving help this causes scandal.

2. On matters of ecology the significant initiatives have almost all come from 'post-Christian' people; when such people seek explicit religious inspiration they look more to India and to the nature religions than to Christianity.

3. As regards participation in decision-making, Church authorities continue to make noble statements which are often grossly contradicted by their own style of exercising authority. (Once again many of the religious congregations are an exception—at least in regard to offering real participation to their members in policy-making; sadly, however, they are not always so generous in opening this participation to the lay people who work with them.)

4. As regards the struggle for the liberation of women: most of those who are committed to this struggle say they experience the

152

Church more as an obstacle or an enemy than as a source of inspiration and hope.

5. Finally, the life-style of almost all of the 'higher' authority figures of the First World Church identifies them as part of the comfortable majority rather than of the marginal people. It is true that there is a certain frugality in the lives of those who hold positions of authority in many of the religious congregations; but, in general, they are still a long way from the life-style of the poor.

In the First World today we are in a situation analogous to that of the Latin American Church prior to its conversion. The official Church is failing people by not articulating their deepest religious instincts *with* them or even *for* them. This is a failure to empower people, just as for centuries the masses of Latin America were deprived by Church leaders of the empowerment they have at last been given in recent years.

When I speak here of being empowered I do not necessarily mean the power to *succeed* in overcoming oppression, or the arms race, or the destruction of the environment, and so on. What is in question comes before success or failure. It is the affirming of people's deepest religious instincts. For instance, people already sense in their hearts that it is a blatant contradiction of the Christian faith to have the Earth permanently threatened by nuclear obliteration, or to discriminate against a person because she is a woman, or to leave anyone helpless before the security forces. The 'empowerment' they need is simply the ability to articulate explicitly such deep Christian instincts.

This kind of power inspires people to action but does not give any guarantee of immediate success. In Latin America there is no indication that effective liberation for the mass of the people is just around the corner. Similarly, there is no assurance that our political, economic, and social structures would be rapidly changed if Church leaders in the First World began to empower Christians (and others) by helping them to develop an authentic spirituality of peace, ecology, participation, and sexual equality. But at least an enormously rich source of inspiration would be available for those who hunger for a coherent articulation of what the Spirit is saying in their hearts.

Theology as Domination

If theology is not deliberately used to *give* power to people then it will almost certainly be used to *take away* power from them; there is no middle way. I have been trying to show how theology can be used to give power to people, how it can become a liberating force in the Church and in society. Now I want to go on to say something about dominating power and about how theology can be used to dominate and oppress people.

Dominating power is power over people. It interferes with their freedom and responsibility. If I am dominating you then I am attempting to deprive you of a part of your human responsibility and dignity—and therefore of a fundamental part of your very humanity. In dominating *you* I am also depriving *myself* of part of my own humanity, because I am acting in an inhuman manner.

Domination takes place in all the different spheres of human life—economic, political, sexual, cultural, and religious. The misuse of theology is just one particular form of cultural-religious domination. But it is particularly obnoxious because it is done under the guise of helping people to understand their Christian faith. It takes different forms:

1. Unchristian Theologies

In certain cases people are persuaded to believe something that contradicts their deepest human and Christian instincts. One classical example is the theology and spirituality preached in Latin America for over four centuries; religious instruction and liturgy were used, on the one hand, to justify the exploitation and oppression carried out by Spanish and Portuguese settlers; and, on the other hand, to convince the oppressed people that their suffering was the will of God.

More recent examples can be found in South Africa today; there one finds a theology and spirituality that are used either to justify the apartheid system itself or to justify the failure of some Christians to challenge it effectively. The authors of the *Kairos Document* identify what they call a blasphemous and heretical 'State Theology' and a 'Church Theology' and spirituality that they consider to be inadequate, misleading, and even 'totally unChristian'.[2]

154

Coming closer to home, I think of the distorted theology of sexuality that was preached at parish missions and school retreats during my teenage years. I realise that many of those who passed on this kind of spirituality were themselves victims of it. So it would be unfair to blame them for the harm they did, especially to young girls and boys who needed help in learning to develop warm and respectful relationships with each other, and in coming to appreciate the gift of their sexuality. But, with the benefit of hindsight, I do not think it is an exaggeration to say that the theology and spirituality we were offered in this sphere of life was quite unChristian.

2. 'Trotted Out' Theology

There is another way in which theology is misused—one that happens so frequently that we may find it difficult even to recognise it as a theological domination. What happens is that preachers or theologians trot out some traditional formula which is presented as 'the truth'. There may be nothing wrong with the content of the theology. But it is imposed without giving people any real opportunity to appropriate it personally or articulate it for themselves.

This deprivation is a form of domination. It denies people their right as humans and as Christians to give personal expression to their deepest values, hopes, and concerns. Furthermore, it robs them of the life, excitement, and inspiration which, as I pointed out above, come from such personal theological activity. It deprives the Christian people of a most important source for the nourishment of their faith. Finally, it leaves them dependent and open to manipulation because they have not learned to articulate their own personal and community religious experience.

3. Ideological Use of Religious Terms

A further abuse of theology occurs when theologians or other Church authorities continue to use certain religious or theological terms in a way that obscures the truth. For instance, to apply the word 'vocation' almost exclusively to priests, nuns, and brothers gives the impression that lay people do not also have a call from God. Some of the religious language used about priests and bishops is of this kind. The priest is still presented at times as 'another Christ' in a way that suggests that this is not

155

true of a lay person. The title 'vicar of Christ' is given to the pope without advertance to the fact that this title could also be given to others—and especially to the person who is hungry, sick, imprisoned, or a stranger (Mt 25:35–40). Scriptural terms that refer to Christ are glibly borrowed to glorify priests—e.g. 'a priest forever according to the order of Melchizedek'. Or people speak of the Last Supper as the first ordination of priests without taking account of the great fluidity that existed in ministry in the early Church. I am afraid that it must be said that this amounts to an ideological use of theology. Unconsciously or half-consciously it is being used to reinforce the privileged position of a particular individual or group.

4. Restricting Theology

The final form of theological domination which I wish to mention is one that attacks the very process of doing theology as a communal participative process—at least when it is done by ordinary 'unqualified' people. One of the most subtle ways in which this kind of theological domination takes place is in the restriction of the word 'theology' itself to the kind of study that can only be carried out by 'experts'. Not long ago I heard a well-known Church leader being interviewed on radio. He was asked to comment on a suggestion made by a highly articulate woman politician that the time had come for the Catholic Church to introduce women priests. He dismissed this opinion as unworthy of serious consideration on the grounds that the woman was not a theologian. Such a restriction on the use of the word 'theologian' gives the impression that those who do not have an academic qualification in theology do not have worthwhile theological insights and therefore have little to contribute to the formulation of Church politics. In my opinion this is a serious mistake.

The nub of the question is whether those who hold authority in the Church are prepared to trust the 'ordinary' Christian people. Do they dare to allow them to reflect and take a personal stand in regard to religious and moral values? I think they cannot afford *not* to take this risk. The fact is that if Church leaders and theologians attempt to impose Christian values on people they will be actually betraying these very values. In an attempt to protect people they will be denying them the freedom that is part of their Christian call.

156

Lay people have much to gain from programmes that enable them to clarify and express their deepest beliefs and values. If Church leaders wish to make an option for the poor, then one important part of it must be a commitment to support and foster such programmes. For at present most lay people are 'poor' in the sense that they are more or less deprived of the encouragement to reflect on their Christian faith and experience. Frequently they are not trusted to do so; perhaps theologians or Church leaders are afraid that the faith of 'unqualified' lay people could be undermined by personal reflection that is not carefully controlled. But the urge to do theology is not inimical to the faith; it is rather a fundamental part of faith. A theology that is imposed makes slaves of people. A theology that is drawn out of people's own Christian experience by sensitive facilitation helps to set them free to be fully Christian, fully human, fully alive.

Section Two: The Option of Theological Colleges

In the previous section I suggested that 'ordinary' Christians have the right to articulate for themselves the faith that is in them, and that ministers of the Church and theologians have a duty to facilitate them in doing so. In this section I want to develop this point further, by looking at its implications for those Church institutions which have the task of teaching theology. The institutional Church must face up to the challenge of adapting existing structures and practices to meet the present needs of the Christian community; and one of the most urgent of these needs is the development of spirituality and theology both *for* and *by* 'ordinary' Christians. I suggest that the people running theological colleges are called to make a major 'option for the poor' by showing a special preference for 'ordinary' Christians as distinct from specialised theologians.

A Challenge

Take the case of a married couple who are 'going through a bad patch' in their relationship. They are looking for some 'expert' to help them find a Christian answer to their difficulty. This help could have come from one of two people. The first possible 'expert' has spent twelve years studying philosophy, theology, and canon law in various seminaries and theological institutes. He was awarded his doctorate for a 400-page dissertation in which he examined the views of 145 Scholastic theologians about what kind of liquid is valid matter for baptism. He now works in a Church marriage tribunal and teaches canon law in a seminary. The other possible helper is a nurse, married to a former carpenter who is now unemployed. Having devoted twenty years of her life to rearing her family she has had more time in recent years for service to the community. So she has trained as a marriage counsellor and has done various short courses in theology.

I am not asking the reader to decide which of these two helpers is likely to be of most help to the couple in difficulty with their marriage. For that depends to a great extent on the character of the two possible counsellors and the nature of the problem. But this case raises serious questions, which should be put to those who own and operate theological institutes: Is it right for the Christian community to allocate its limited resources in such a way that the priest gets so much of them while the lay women get so little? Is it not likely that more help would be forthcoming to couples in trouble with their marriages if a lot more of the time and energy of the staff of Church institutes of theology were devoted to people like the committed lay woman?

The Purpose of Theological Institutes
Having posed the question in terms of an example, I want now to look at it in more general terms by examining the purpose of Church institutes of theology. I think the purpose is to serve the Christian community in two ways:
—by training ministers.
—by promoting research.
I shall look at each of these in turn.

In most of our Churches the trained ministers are male clerics. The resources of very many theological institutes are spent mainly on educating this group rather than others. In fact a very high proportion of the educational resources of the Church as a whole is spent on training and 'renewing' the clergy. There is an obvious need to devote resources to this important work. But is there not a certain lack of proportion, perhaps even of justice, in the fact that such a small proportion of the resources goes to the people like the married woman in the example above?

The cost to the Christian community of the education of a priest or minister is in the region of £30,000 in Europe and $50,000 in North America. For each priest ordained in the Catholic Church in Western countries there are about two lay people who studied with him but left the seminary before ordination or left the priesthood afterwards. The cost to the Christian community of the theological education of each of them may have been between £10,000 and £30,000 in Europe or between $20,000 and $50,000 in America. While it is good to have such a reservoir of theologically educated people in the Church, we must also ask whether this represents an equitable allocation of resources. There are two ways of looking at this cost. On the one hand, we may say that the *real* cost of the education of each priest has to be double or treble the sums given above. Alternatively, we may say that very large sums of money are devoted to providing theological education for large number of lay people, of whom relatively few are subsequently involved in any active Church ministry. Meanwhile many other active lay leaders—people like the woman in the above example—lack the resources for serious theological education. It is true that most theological colleges now provide courses for lay people; but courses are still designed mainly to meet the needs of clergy.

One effect of the specialised training of the clergy is that they become a privileged group.[3] Their position of privilege gives them power. They often use this power in a way that widens the gap between themselves, the privileged ones, and the under-privileged—and this can easily happen even when they are not trying to abuse their position.

This kind of imbalance is a good example of what is meant by 'structural injustice'. All Christians are called to overcome such injustices—in fact that is precisely what is entailed in saying that the Church and its leaders are called to make an option for the poor.[4] It seems clear that an option in favour of 'the poor' in this situation would lead to the provision of much more extensive ministry training for lay people who have committed themselves to putting their talents at the service of the community.

Those who own or staff theological institutes are therefore called to shift their priorities. It is not simply a question of making courses available to lay leaders. In order to make theology widely accessible to laity there is a need for a shift in both the *content* of many courses and in the *methodology* used. A much more experiential approach is called for, one that finds a starting-point in the Christian experience of those who take part in the course. (Such a change of approach would be of benefit to those who are preparing for the ordained ministry as well as the lay leaders.) Changes in the programmes would have to be complemented by some change in the priorities that decide who receives financial support while studying in theological institutes.

We can now go on to look at the question of research. The research done in institutes of theology has mainly been done by male clerics. Like any other group, we clerics have our own blind spots. Though our aim is to discover objective truth it is more or less inevitable that the end-product will largely be the truth as seen by us male clerical theologians. Furthermore, we tend to have our own priorities in choosing topics for research. The long-term effect is an exacerbation of the existing imbalance between clerics and laity.

An option for the poor would require significant changes. To open up research to the less privileged would involve changing many of our present presuppositions, e.g.
—presuppositions about what experience counts as making one qualified to do research, and therefore about who can expect financial and moral support;
—presuppositions about what kind of operations count as research;
—presuppositions regarding the groups for whose benefit research is carried out;
—presuppositions about how the benefits are fed back into the community.
The effect of all this would be, of course, some change in priorities—with more attention paid to topics that are neglected at present and lower priority given to areas of research that are presently considered important. The resultant loss would be outweighed by the opening up of largely untouched areas of theological research.

Who Decides?

Institutes of theology are owned not by those who staff them but by hierarchies and religious bodies of various kinds. To implement the kind of changes suggested here would obviously require the backing of the owners of the institutes.

Suppose the owners of an institute are a religious congregation or group of congregations, or a body of bishops. They may be inclined to say that they are bound to give first priority to the education of new members for their own religious congregations or of young priests to serve in their dioceses. But to say this is to beg the question. In effect it is equivalent to saying: 'What we have, we hold.' Such an attitude is a clear contradiction of an option for the poor.

Because of the considerable challenge involved, there is a danger that both the *owners* and the *staff* of theological institutes might dodge responsibility; each group could tacitly assume that the initiative should be taken by the other group. The fact is that the changes needed are so difficult that initiatives would have to come from *both* sides. Certainly, the present staff have a key role to play in exploring the options and in devising and suggesting ways of phasing in the changes. Perhaps the best initiative that could be taken by the owners of the institutes would be to appoint to positions of responsibility theologians and administrators who are willing to face up to this major challenge.

First Steps

Many of the practical difficulties involved are lessened when the directors and staffs of theological institutes are willing to make use of more effective modes of adult education. Notable steps have already been taken in some theological colleges towards getting away from the older almost exclusive reliance on the lecture system. This needs to be taken further. As colleges adopt a more experiential model of learning they will have to help their staff to become proficient in using the newer methods. They will also need to take on more lay staff—women and men. These changes will enable the colleges to adapt fairly easily to educating various categories of Christian for a greater variety of ministries in the community; and they will also be open to a far greater variety in research.

This approach makes it possible to have a much more mixed group of learners working together. To provide a theological education is not like feeding a homogeneous batch of chickens the same chicken-feed. We can have a very diverse group of Christians who are being facilitated to learn at least as much from each other as from the official resource person. I shall develop these ideas more fully in the next chapter of this book.

I have said practically nothing here about option for the poor in its most obvious sense, namely, siding with those who are economically exploited or politically marginalised. I have concentrated attention on one particular aspect of option for the poor. In some respects it is a relatively minor one. But I have focused on it because it follows on immediately from the crucial question dealt with in the first part of this chapter—that of enabling Christians to play an active part in developing their own spirituality and theology.

There is a real danger that committed staff members of theological institutes would spend a lot of time and energy in a somewhat theoretical 'covering' of the topic of 'option for the poor' in the economic and political spheres, while failing to advert to this other aspect—one that lies much closer at hand. It would be overstating the case to call this an instance of seeing the speck in another person's eye while ignoring the beam in one's own eye. However, one might see it as a case of trying to remove the beam from the eye of the other while ignoring the speck in one's own eye—and that is by no means an easy thing to do!

8

Justice in Formation

HOW DO ADULT Christians develop and nourish their spirituality? Theological education plays a part—but it is only one part of a much larger process. The person needs to explore—intellectually and experientially—what it means to be a believer. There is need, too, for the person to take on commitments. This, in turn calls for the development of virtues and patterns of behaviour— and, very frequently, for a healing of the spirit from the wounds of the past. While engaging in this whole process the person needs to be animated, facilitated, inspired, challenged and supported by sensitive, wise and experienced Christian mentors. The word 'education' is too limited to cover all that is involved, and the word 'training' is quite unsuitable. So, in the English-speaking world, the word 'formation' has come into use over the past twenty years to cover this whole process. At first it was used mainly to refer to the period of preparation for those who wished to join a religious congregation or community. Six or seven years ago the word began to be extended to the time of preparation for the priesthood. But it is only within the past two or three years that it has begun to be used fairly widely in English-speaking countries to cover what used to be called programmes of 'education' or 'training' for lay Christians.

At present the traditional programmes of formation for priests and for members of religious communities are being re-designed in a fairly radical way. At the same time some attempts are being made to design courses for lay people which will provide them not merely with theological education but also with a *formation* that is appropriate to their situation. Sadly, however, most Christians are quite unfamiliar with the word 'formation'. This indicates that both Church leaders and the Christian community still have a long way to go before it is taken for granted that lay leaders need formation programmes just as much as clergy or members of religious communities—and that a crucial aspect of their formation is to enable them to take part in the formation of others.

In this chapter I hope to look at some models of formation with special reference to how the virtue of justice should be incorporated in a formation programme. One aspect of this is how people should be educated to respond to injustice in society. But equally important is the question of how the resources of the Christian community should be used justly to meet the formation needs of lay people as well as of clergy and members of religious communities.

A major problem that affects the Churches in much of the Western world is, on the one hand, that of formation programmes without people to make use of them and, on the other, that of people without programmes available to them. In an incisive analysis of this issue, Martin Kennedy notes that clergy and members of religious communities have a highly organised system of training with plenty of resources available for the work. But the burning question for those who maintain this system is how to get people into the system; for the number of people in the Western world who are entering these programmes is dwindling. Seen from this point of view the problem is *a system without people*. But Kennedy goes on to present another way of looking at the situation. There are, he points out, lots of people who want to live out their Christian commitment very fully as lay people; but they are not provided with roles and training to call forth and sustain that commitment.

> The burning question here is: 'How are we going to imagine and put in place ways that enable lay people to take up a vital role in the life of the Church?' The problem is *a people without a system*.[1]

In the light of this analysis it must be said that those who speak of 'a crisis of vocations' in the Western Churches are naming the problem wrongly. It is not right to restrict the word 'vocation' almost exclusively to the call to be a cleric or a member of a religious community. To do so suggests that lay people do not have a vocation. A vocation is a sense of a personal call by God to take up a particular way of life and a particular ministry in the Church; and an increasing number of

164

lay people have experienced such a 'vocation' in recent years. So it is inaccurate and unjust to speak of 'a drop in vocations' in Western countries in recent years. In fact all the evidence is that there has been an *increase* in vocations—provided we give the word 'vocation' its truly Christian meaning. We do not have a shortage of 'vocations'. What we have is a significant change in the nature of the role to which many committed Christians are being called.

At present people are feeling themselves called to a great variety of ministries in the Church. There is need for formation for these ministries—to *prepare* people for them and to provide those who exercise them with *ongoing support*. It is obvious that there must be a difference between the type and degree of formation required for, say, a person who takes on the task of distributing the Eucharist on Sundays, and that required by a full-time minister of the Gospel. But there is no Christian justification for beginning with a very sharp distinction between clergy and laity and presuming that the formation programme for each category should be different except where it can be proved that they should be similar.

On the contrary, what we find in the Gospels is that those who are called to be *apostles* are first of all *disciples*. Their formation programme is a programme in discipleship. As this progresses, an apostolic quality is discovered to be implicit in discipleship. In calling some of his followers to be apostles Jesus was not simply adding on something new from outside; he was ratifying and nourishing a vocation that had unfolded from within the experience of being his follower. Similarly today, a good formation programme for Christian believers will lead many of them to recognise a call to ministry as part of their response. And by far the largest part of any programme of formation for ministry must be formation as disciples of Jesus.

This suggests that to a considerable extent there should be joint formation programmes for committed lay people, clergy, and members of religious communities. In what I have to say about formation programmes in the remainder of this chapter I am not referring to the very general formation that has to be given to all Christians. Rather I have in mind the more specialised formation required by clergy, by members of religious communities, and by highly committed lay leaders such as youth

165

ministers, lay missionaries, religious educators, and those who devote themselves to the Christian ministry of counselling or spiritual direction.

Jesus' Approach to Formation

In order to provide a basis for evaluation of the present models of formation it may be useful to look briefly at what the Gospels tell us about the way Jesus formed his followers. A first point to note is that Jesus did not swamp his followers with a lot of theory; their formation was mostly done 'in the field'. A second point is that he clearly respected their personal responsibility. He did not demand mindless conformity. Rather he engaged in serious dialogue with them—e.g. 'Who do you say I am?' (Mt 16:15); and he encouraged them (e.g. 'Take heart'— Mt 14:27) while at the same time challenging them (e.g. 'Let the greatest among you become as the youngest . . . '—Lk 22:26). Neither did Jesus impose a regime of severe discipline on his followers— cf. 'your disciples do not fast'(Mt 9:14).

In this respect the Gospel accounts give solid support to those who, over the past twenty years, have largely abandoned the model of formation that was widely used in seminaries and novitiates a generation ago. That older model was one that stressed *conformity* as one of its highest values. The neophyte was taught to conform to a discipline imposed 'from above'. In some cases the discipline was very largely an external one, accepted by the student or novice out of fear of being caught. In other cases the discipline was internalised—and at times this was done through a process that came perilously close to the kind of 'brainwashing' used by various cult-groups today.

Alongside this practical training, the person in training in the past was also given a considerable body of theory. This came almost exclusively in the form of lectures, through which information was lodged in the bank of the student's brain with little opportunity to assess it critically, or even to relate it to one's personal life. Here again the value was one of conformity; the aim was that the ideas and thought patterns of the trainee should conform to the received wisdom as expressed in the manuals of theology and the handbooks of spirituality.

The approach of Jesus had much more in common with what we may call the 'Apprenticeship Model' of formation. In its

166

simplest form this involves an expert and a learner. The 'expert' may be an electrician, a surgeon, a priest, or a hermit. The subject is learned mainly 'on the ground' in a practical way. But there may also be quite a lot of theoretical work to be done by the learner in order to be able to benefit from the practical instruction. The learner is frequently introduced not merely to a body of knowledge and a set of skills, but also to a whole way of life.

The *main location* of the formation offered by Jesus was the very busy world in which he was exercising his ministry. Clearly he did not consider that his followers needed to be cut off from the world because there was so much evil in it—or even because the pace of their life was so frenetic. However, the Gospels make it clear that he ensured that they were not swamped by the burden of their ministry to others. There were many times when Jesus felt it necessary to *withdraw for a time* into a secluded place. He felt the need to take time and space both for himself (e.g. Mt 14:23) and for his companions:

'Come away by yourselves to a lonely place, and rest a while.' For many were coming and going, and they had no leisure even to eat. (Mk 6:31)

In the Gospels we find that Jesus sent his followers out on trial runs, to carry out a healing and teaching ministry like his own. His purpose, we may presume, was twofold: to spread his 'Good News' more widely, and to prepare his followers to continue his ministry when he was no longer with them. It is significant that they were not sent out as isolated individuals but in little teams: 'He called to him the twelve, and began to send them out two by two . . .' (Mk 6:7); 'After this the Lord appointed seventy others, and sent them on ahead of him, two by two . . .' (Lk 10:1). When they came back they shared their experiences with him and he brought them off into a secluded place for further reflection with him (Mk 6:30-31).

Facing Failure

It would be quite easy to overlook one of the most remarkable features of the formation programme of Jesus, namely, that it continued right through his rejection, his suffering and his death—and beyond. The Gospels make it very clear that Jesus realised that he would be made to suffer and die. They also

167

indicate that he considered it essential that his followers appreciate how important this was for his ministry (e.g. Mt 16:21). Jesus was willing to face the human failure of his mission *in front of* his followers—and even to be crucified in front of any of them who could stay with him through his suffering. Not only that; he was even willing to admit his need for their support during his darkest hour, and to express his disappointment when they failed him in his time of weakness: 'Could you not watch with me one hour?' (Mt 26:40).

All this indicates that Jesus was not content with a conventional apprenticeship model. He was not to be seen as 'the expert' who always had things under his control—at least not in the obvious sense. It is true, of course, that the evangelists (especially John and, to a lesser extent, Luke) felt it important to show that in another sense Jesus remained in control, precisely because he was able to draw success out of his failure and find a meaning in his death, e.g. John 18:6: 'When he said to them "I am he," they drew back and fell to the ground.' (cf. Lk 22:51). But this was not control exercised by the 'expert' according to the standards of the world; rather it is recognised as success only by a wisdom that challenges worldly standards; it is only by the gift of faith that the Christian can see a Divine success in the failure of the mission of Jesus and his execution as a criminal.

Accompaniment and Facilitation

Increasingly today the term used by formation people to describe their work and approach is that they are 'accompanying' those who are in formation. What this means in practice is that the people in formation are *facilitated* to make their own decisions, based on their own experiences—of prayer, of com-munity life, and of pastoral involvement. This goes hand in hand with a good deal of spiritual direction which may be formal or informal. Formation programmes in preparation for priesthood or membership of religious communities are not entirely non-directive. They have a greater or lesser amount of more academic input; and some measure of discipline is also required of the participants.

Where formation programmes are a prerequisite for admission to any Church ministry or for entry to a religious community, justice enters into the relationship between those who direct the programme and those for whom it has been designed. It is

168

a matter of justice to give those who are being 'formed' the opportunity to take part in designing their programme of formation. Justice also requires that we be fully truthful in the language we use. For instance, those who are responsible for the formation of others should be very careful about the way they speak of 'accompanying' those who are in formation. The word is ambiguous. It could easily give the impression that those in formation are merely being 'accompanied' and not being assessed according to some criteria of those in authority. The use of such a non-judgmental word, combined with the reality of ongoing assessment, could easily be deceptive and manipulative. It would be unjust not to make clear to those in formation the criteria that are used to evaluate their progress; unjust to leave them at the mercy of arbitrary judgments about their suitability.

Formation programmes in preparation for the priesthood or for joining a religious community make use of two quite different versions of the 'facilitation' approach to formation:

—There is what we may call 'the seclusion version', where the aim is to isolate the people in formation to a very considerable extent from secular life for several months or longer, in order to give them an intense undisturbed experience of spirituality, and time for discernment. During this time their psychological and spiritual growth is facilitated by those who are responsible for implementing the formation programme.

—In sharp contrast to this, there is 'the exposure version', where those who are being 'formed' are sent out for a period of immersion in demanding pastoral situations. For instance, they may go to work with drug addicts or homeless people. Or they may become involved in consciousness-raising or other justice issues. The period of exposure is followed by a return to a relatively secluded environment in which there is the opportunity for 'debriefing', i.e. for reflection on the experience. From the point of view of those who are in charge of the formation programme, reflection on the exposure experience is at least as important as the exposure itself. Those who are responsible for the formation programme will see their task as facilitating this reflection.

In recent times the formation programmes in preparation for the priesthood or for membership of a religious community generally make use of both these approaches. Periods of intense

169

exposure are usually preceded and followed by periods of seclusion. And a fairly small but regular amount of pastoral ministry (and reflection) is inserted into the long years that are devoted mainly to study and community life.

In this model, those who are in charge of formation see their role primarily as facilitators. In order to be good facilitators they may feel that they should hold back from sharing in the same pastoral involvement as those whom they are facilitating. There is a certain one-way character to the relationship between a therapist and a client or patient: the therapist identifies with the difficulties of the client but this is not reciprocated. In somewhat the same way (though to a lesser extent) whose who are directing the formation programme of others may feel a need to maintain a certain element of reserve in relation to them.

Did Jesus 'accompany' his followers in the sense envisaged by those engaged in religious formation today? I think it would be more accurate to say that he invited *them* to accompany *him* rather than the other way round—cf. 'Come and see' (Jn 1:39), 'Follow me' (Mt 4:19) and 'Will you also go away?' (Jn 6:67). What emerges is that Jesus had a formation programme which involved sharing with those whom he invited or allowed to follow him—sharing his daily life, his meals, his prayer, and his ministry of healing and teaching.

It is clear that Jesus went beyond the conception of facilitation or accompaniment which I have described above. He made no effort to maintain the kind of reserve that would ensure that his own concerns did not intrude on the personal development of his followers. On the contrary, he integrated into their formation programme his own struggle against weakness and failure. He saw that their formation would be advanced by their having to cope with his failure and by his asking for their support in his weakness.

A Christian Discipleship Model of Formation

A study of the example of Jesus should encourage those in charge of today's formation programmes to make a radical appraisal of present models of formation. Like Jesus himself, they should be actively involved in initiating their charges into pastoral ministry. And like him, they should not try to cover up their own weaknesses and struggles.

170

If we take seriously the example of Jesus, there is a very good case for doing more formation 'in the field', making use of elements from the apprenticeship model. This means, in practice, that there would be far more scope than in the past for highly motivated lay people to share formation programmes with those who are preparing for the full-time ministry or for membership of religious communities. The gap between formation and 'ordinary' life would be greatly reduced.

Care would have to be taken to ensure that the work of the ministry itself was not allowed to take precedence over the task of formation. The obvious way to lessen this danger would be to follow the example of Jesus in ensuring that there are periods of withdrawal for rest and reflection.

It would be glib to suggest that today's formation programmes should be simply identical with that of Jesus. Apart from the differences of time and situation there is the more important point that formation people are not aiming to produce disciples of *themselves* as Jesus was; rather they are called to be co-disciples of Jesus, *alongside* those who are in formation. This means that formation cannot be seen simply as apprenticeship in the conventional sense. It must be clear that, as disciples, those directing the formation programme are themselves in a learning position, not experts or models.

Those in charge of formation should not see facilitation as the supremely important element in their 'accompaniment' of those in formation. Facilitation should not, of course, be downgraded entirely, since it is obviously vital in helping people to learn from their experience and to take responsibility for their lives. But if formation people give priority to facilitation they may want to do their own learning mainly out of sight of those whose formation they are 'accompanying'; they may want to be available precisely as facilitators—with the kind of psychic distance that is thought to promote such a relationship. But it may be more valuable if they share their lives and ministry openly as co-disciples with those who are being 'formed'. (However, it is useful—and often necessary—for those who are in charge of a formation programme to have a counsellor of their own with whom they work out their strictly *personal* problems, rather than impose these on the group with whom they are working.)

171

An Integral Ministry of Justice

To follow the example of Jesus in formation work means giving priority to pastoral ministry. But what kind of pastoral ministry is most appropriate? Obviously it should be work that is relevant to today's world. It is important that people in formation should come to understand the socio-cultural and politico-economic situation of the region in which they are working. And it is also important that they learn to have real sympathy for the people among whom they work. But the ultimate purpose of committed Christians being inserted into the world is in order to share in Christ's ministry of *saving* the world. So it is important that the experience of pastoral ministry should not simply involve helping people to cope with the world as it is. It should not consist merely in visiting hospitals or working in institutions which provide food and shelter for 'drop outs'.

A significant amount of the pastoral ministry involved in formation programmes should be concerned with helping to transform the world. In this way those in formation will learn to share in Christ's work of bringing into being a new world or, in Biblical terms, 'the Kingdom'. In practice, this means that people in formation should be involved from an early stage in work for the promotion of justice, peace, and the integrity of creation.

Some experience of involvement in a justice ministry is an indispensable part of any worthwhile formation programme. We need to learn how to work for justice for and with 'the poor'. To whom does this term 'the poor' refer? Some would restrict the meaning so that it covers only those who are economically or politically deprived. Others extend the term to cover rich people who are 'spiritually poor'—and at this stage almost everybody is covered. In my opinion 'the poor' in this context includes all groups who are left relatively powerless—not merely those who are economically deprived or politically marginalised but also people who suffer discrimination on the basis of gender or race or culture—or (in Church matters) because they are not clergy.

Justice is not merely a matter of ensuring a fair balance in the distribution of the goods of the world. It also includes respect for fundamental human rights. And one fundamental right which is a key to most other rights is the right to participate in making decisions that affect oneself and one's community. So, under the

172

heading 'justice ministry' we should include any programme which sets out to promote a more participative style of decision-making in society or in the Church itself.

In recent years it has become more and more clear that ecological issues are an integral and crucial part of the justice agenda. A good deal of modern so-called development is really a matter of the plundering by a relatively small number of people of resources which had been available for the benefit of all—and of future generations. Closely linked to the new and urgent concern for ecology is work for disarmament and other forms of peace work.[2]

Solidarity

One crucial reason for integrating a justice ministry into formation programmes is to give the participants the experience of 'solidarity with the poor'. The Christian, like Christ, is called to be in solidarity with those who are victims, or who have a less privileged place in society. Solidarity involves shared understanding and values, leading to shared commitment. But, as I pointed out in chapter 5 above, prior to all of this there is need for some measure of shared *experiences*.

Sharing in the daily life experiences of disadvantaged people provides the basis for a degree of shared affective response—that is, for feelings and spontaneous reactions similar to those of 'the poor'. This does not mean that if I am in solidarity with 'the poor' I will always respond or even feel exactly as they do: for my spontaneous responses are largely shaped by my background, my education and my previous experiences. But the effect of sharing something of the lives and experiences of marginalised people is that some part of me at least will reverberate with the feelings of rejection, resentment, alienation, and hopelessness that are so common among the victims of society. I may also find within me an echo of the generosity, the spontaneous compassion and the hope beyond all hope that frequently characterise the lives of poor people.

One of the biggest problems in modern times is the widespread assumption made by those who hold power in society and the Church that they are making decisions on the basis of objective knowledge of the situation of those who are powerless. But the planners and decision-makers who claim to know the

173

situation ignore the fact that one's view of reality changes with the perspective from which it is viewed. The view from the bottom is by no means the same as the view from the top of society. For instance, the experience which squatters have of the police and the law is very different from the experience of property owners; and these different experiences give rise to two quite different understandings of law enforcement. Only when we share the experience of disadvantaged people can we have any chance of sharing their understanding of injustice. Not a purely intellectual understanding but one that has the texture of the life experience of the people involved—their pain, their anger, and the hope that keeps them going.

A member of a religious community or a seminarian is a person in a relatively privileged position: so too are many of those who feel called to a role of lay leadership in the Church. Suppose such a person shares some of the experiences of victims of injustice. The result of this should be that his or her affective responses would be more authentically Christian—by which I mean more like those of Christ himself. What would such a response be in practice? I think it would be an amalgam of three distinct affective elements:

—a compassion for those who are suffering the injustice;
—anger directed against whoever and whatever is causing the injustice;
—a yearning for redress, stemming from a real hope that the injustice can and will be overcome.

Out of this affective soil can grow an authentically Christian *understanding* of the nature of justice and a *commitment* to struggle to bring it about. The lesson of the Bible, a lesson that is slowly being learned by the Church, is that transformation of the world will not come about from the top down; for it is not in the interest of those who are wealthy and powerful to relinquish their positions of privilege. God has chosen those who are poor and powerless, those who seem foolish in the eyes of the powerful, to be special instruments of healing, transformation and salvation. If we wish to love the world in God's way then we will freely choose to work in solidarity with 'the lowly ones'. Our aim will be to empower them to become agents of change in society. Our dedication to justice will be imbued with love. We must not allow the commitment to justice to be set over against the effort

174

to love others. Quite the contrary; for the way to be loving in the public or institutional sphere is to work for justice.

The Danger of Excessive Specialisation

It is not easy to integrate a commitment to a justice ministry with the other values of the formation programme. So those in charge of formation may be tempted to hand over responsibility for this aspect of the programme to just one or two members of the formation team, leaving it to them to specialise in matters of justice. That would be a mistake. All members of the formation team need to be involved in some degree in the pastoral ministry of justice. If it is left to people other than the main formation people then it may well be played down,[3] or there may be tensions between those who are in charge of different aspects of the formation programme. The most effective way in which those who are being 'formed' can learn to integrate justice values with other formation values is for them to see before their eyes the struggle of the members of the formation team to achieve such an integration in their own lives.

But how can formation people be expected to be competent not only in formation but also in matters of justice? I would reply; they cannot afford *not* to be. For they are not competent formation people at all if they have specialised only in the 'personal' dimension of spirituality. Of its very nature, spirituality has a public dimension as well. All members of the formation team have to take this seriously in their own lives; otherwise they are likely to pass on a truncated approach to spirituality to those whom they are 'accompanying'.

Some formation people argue that their top priority must be to attain that spiritual freedom and inner detachment which are essential to anybody whose task is to be a spiritual guide or director for others; hence they dare not get very involved in a justice ministry which would put them under great spiritual pressure. In response to this argument I would agree that they must do their best to achieve spiritual freedom—but they should do so while following the example of Jesus who did this during a challenging pastoral ministry. They are not dealing adequately with the justice dimension of formation if their only involvement is to facilitate a reflection by *others* on the experience of being involved in a justice ministry. What is required is more

175

like an apprenticeship system—but one that incorporates a lot of reflection and facilitation.

I am not saying that the members of the formation team need to have a full-time involvement in a justice ministry. That would make their task as formation people almost impossible. What is required is a *significant* involvement—so that it has a notable impact on their own lives. They must have personal experience of the kind of difficulties that arise for people in such a ministry. This personal experience must not be just something in the past; those who are being formed must see the members of the formation team struggling to maintain spiritual freedom despite the pressures. Regular failure is an indication that the person is unsuited to be on the formation team. But occasional failure may be turned into a real advantage if the person does not try to 'cover up' for weakness and failure in front of those who are in formation.

Team Ministry

It is important that the pastoral experience both of those who are being educated for ministry and of those who are directing the formation programme should be that of a *team* ministry. One reason for this is to follow the example of Jesus. But there are also more practical reasons. The team can provide support for its members—and challenge as well. Furthermore, learning to work in a team, respecting the feelings and views of others, is itself an important item on the justice agenda. Another practical advantage is that the team can be organised in a way that allows its members some flexibility. It will be possible to make allowances for occasional absences of those being 'formed' or of those responsible for formation; for both groups will have other commitments to meet.[4]

There is need for plenty of team meetings after the example of Jesus and his first disciples. These meetings should include:
—evaluation of the effectiveness of the work in transforming society,
—evaluation of the teamwork of those taking part,
—evaluation of the psychological and religious effects on those engaged in the ministry.

One of the most powerful arguments for a team ministry is that it makes it much easier to design formation programmes where lay people, clergy (or candidates for priesthood), and members of religious communities can all have a real experience of solidarity in working together. This is one place where important steps can be taken to correct the balance in the distribution of resources in the Church; lay people can share in the resources available to clergy and religious communities. It is a matter of justice how the available Church resources are allocated between different groups who are all in need of formation. We have to consider whether the resources of expertise, time, energy, buildings, and finance are fairly divided between the three main categories—clerics, members of religious communities, and laity. If one or two of these groups are being ignored or not given sufficient resources, then justice requires that the balance be rectified.

If it becomes evident that the laity are being neglected, this does not necessarily require that we skimp on the resources offered to the other two groups; it might be more helpful all round—and relatively painless as well—to ensure a more equitable distribution by redesigning some of the formation programmes for clergy or religious communities in such a way as to open up parts of them (at least) to emergent lay leaders. One way in which this can be put into practice is by forming and training mixed teams, where lay people work on equal terms with clergy and members of religious communities.

A further justice issue arises here. It concerns the use of language—specifically, the way people apply the word 'religious' as a noun to those people who have taken vows and become members of a religious congregation. This usage is not merely confusing; it is also unjust—for it leaves one with a subliminal impression that other Christians are not religious or are less religious. Just as it is wrong to restrict unduly the meaning of the word 'vocation', so too it is wrong to allow members of religious congregations to have a kind of monopoly of the word 'religious'.

Sharing Resources with Laity

Several years ago some theological colleges, which had been formally or practically reserved to clergy, opened up their courses to lay people. This was an important sharing of theological resources that had previously been available mainly to clerics. It

177

was achieved by making a fairly clear distinction between academic theology and the 'formational aspects' in priestly training. It was assumed at the time that the formational aspects were of no great importance or interest to laity. Today that assumption has to be questioned. We need to go further in the sharing of resources. Many emergent lay leaders have a great need and desire for the kind of 'formational resources' that are made available to clerics and those who enter religious congregations—e.g. spiritual direction, accompaniment, facilitation, programmes of exposure and opportunities for periods of seclusion. In a limited number of situations lay people have been allowed access to such resources *alongside* clerics or members of religious communities. This 'experiment' has proved to be easier to organise than had been expected and the results have been very valuable and exciting for all concerned. What is now required is a further extension of this approach.

I myself have been involved over many years in the training of Christian leaders. My experience has been that formation programmes are most valuable when the group is a mixed one— men and women, laity and clergy and members of religious communities. An objection sometimes raised against mixed programmes is that they have to be so general that they cannot meet the specific needs of the different groups. But, in my experience, whatever might be lost through not dealing with a homogeneous and specialised group (e.g. a group composed entirely of clergy) is more than compensated for by the richness and variety of experience of the mixed group. But, as I pointed out towards the end of the previous chapter, it is necessary to use an experiential model of education if one is to derive benefit from this diversity of Christian experience.

At present there is a wide gulf between the kind of programmes that are offered to committed lay Christians and those available to clergy or members of religious communities. It is unrealistic to think that this gulf will be bridged easily or quickly. So it seems opportune to explore the possibility of adapting and developing existing lay formation programmes, as a step towards the ideal of more integrated formation in the future.

The kind of formation that is widely offered to lay leaders at present often consists of a series of evening lectures once or twice a week over a period of months. It is neither fair nor realistic to

178

expect people to feel qualified and competent to engage in various lay ministries after such meagre courses. Training for ministry has to be taken more seriously than that. On the other hand, nobody could reasonably expect lay leaders to go through the kind of initial formation programmes that are presently required for clergy or for members of religious communities. These are organised according to a pattern that makes them more or less inaccessible to most lay Christians. What is required is a way of making available to all interested members of the Christian community the resources that are currently at the disposal of clergy and members of religious communities. But this needs to be done in such a way that the perceived needs of these latter groups are still met.

A Proposal

Recently I was a member of a small mixed group in which we reflected on our experience of involvement in a variety of formation programmes. We went on to take some tentative steps towards designing a programme of the kind just mentioned, taking account of available resources. I give here a brief summary of some of our tentative conclusions:

—The formation programme needs to be organised at the local or regional level so that participants would normally continue to live in their own homes. On one or two occasions during the programme they would be invited to take part in more intensive residential training sessions for a few days.

—The main purpose of the programme should be to help the participants develop an integral spirituality. In a recent book I have outlined some of the material that might be included.[5]

—It should be integral in approach rather than narrowly religious or 'churchy'. This means it would take account of social and political issues as well as personal and interpersonal ones. It would aim to train the participants to be ministers in all the areas of life where there is need for growth, healing, and transformation.

—A vital element in the programme would be reflection by the participants on their own experience of ministry. This reflection would be deepened by using it as a basis for the study of major issues in today's world and major themes in theology and spirituality.

179

—The ministry in which the participants would be engaged should, ideally, be one which involves the promotion of peace and justice and respect for the environment.

—Participants in the programme would be trained to work as members of mixed teams; and their pastoral experience should be one of working in a team.

—The programme should be experiential and practical, with more emphasis on religion than on theology, and on skills rather than theory. It should be designed to help participants to appreciate and utilise the gifts, education, and skills they *already* have rather than treating them as empty vessels to be filled with new knowledge.

—The programme should be of a kind that would be valuable not only for lay leaders but also for clergy and members of religious communities. Being experiential and skills-oriented, the programme would be one where lay people could work comfortably alongside clergy without feeling patronised by them. It would be one where all participants would soon discover that they have much to learn from the experiences of the others. As such it could be an important step towards the acceptance by clergy of the value of joint formation programmes with laity.

Having looked at existing programmes we were struck by their variety and the element of free competition between the different courses. We concluded that the kind of formation-for-ministry programme outlined above should not be in competition with other popular adult education programmes but should rather be a *follow-up* to them. So the programme would be designed for people who had already taken one of the other courses. This means that the overall formation programme for adults could be seen as having two stages.

The first stage would be any one of a wide variety of existing adult education programmes (e.g. the 'Discovery' programme for young adults, or a training programme for counsellors of the Catholic Marriage Advisory Council, or one of the extension programmes of religious education offered by various colleges). This stage would consist of about 100 'contact-hours', of which three quarters would be working-time and the remainder would be time in which the participants and the organisers would socialise together—partly over snacks and partly on some kind of outing. The period during which this first stage would last would depend, of course, on the level of intensity of the programme. The time might be made up of about thirty sessions, held on one evening each week over the Autumn to Spring period in Western countries, or during the dry season in tropical areas; alternatively, the hundred hours might well be covered in an intensive ten-day workshop.

The second stage would be the kind of programme outlined above. It would be specifically designed as a formation programme for people who, having completed the first stage (in one form or another) want to go on to learn the skills and knowledge appropriate for Christian leaders or ministers. The training offered should be experiential, and tailored to the expressed needs of the particular group. But at the same time we felt that each group should be invited to see the value of ensuring that all such groups would cover roughly the same content—though perhaps in a different order and with varying degrees of emphasis. One advantage of this element of standardisation is that it would make it easier to achieve recognition and accreditation for the formation programme. A further practical advantage is that it would have the effect of building up a corps of trained leaders who could all 'speak the same language' and could therefore more easily work together in teams.

Our experience of working with such people led us to conclude that these emergent leaders would need about 200 contact-hours (in addition to the hundred hours of the first stage) in order to feel reasonably confident as facilitators and resource people working with groups on issues related to human and Christian development. The allocation of this time would depend on circumstance. It could be done in a series of short intensive workshops. (For instance, the leadership training programmes in which I was involved in East and West Africa generally had a series of one-week workshops). But it could also be spread over a two-year period of evening sessions once a week; in this case, however, there should be at least one intensive live-in workshop, to help to bond the group together more effectively. Of the total 200 contact-hours, we felt that about 150 would be working hours. A significant part of the remaining 50 hours should be given over to some such event as a pilgrimage—or perhaps a festival which might have both religious and secular aspects.

181

If we are serious in our commitment to the work of evangelising the world and transforming it by God's creative power, then we need to devote much of our energy to the formation of leaders. Existing formation programmes need to be radically recast if they are to reflect the values and priorities of the Christian agenda today. Perhaps some of the ideas presented there may be of help to those who are able and willing to bring about the changes required. The Church is called by Christ to share in his work of transforming the world. In order to respond to this call it needs constantly to renew itself. An important part of this task of renewal is the provision of adequate formation for all Christians who experience a call to work for the promotion of peace, justice and respect for the Earth which is God's gift to us.

Conclusion

AS I FINISH writing this book I am very aware of the exciting challenge facing the Church today—the challenge of responding to the urgent need of our world and our Earth for justice, peace and respect for the integrity of creation. At the same time I am conscious of how difficult it is for individual Christians and for the Church as a whole to respond effectively to this challenge.

Above all we are blocked by a lack of true leadership. The option of a real alternative to the present world order is not put clearly before the people. Very few government leaders are prepared to take the risk of going against the current, of helping people to see how much they have to gain by exploring the alternatives. We need inspiration if we are to have any hope of changing our present model of development so that it becomes a fair and balanced development for all instead of an unbalanced, unjust, and ecologically exploitative development that favours a minority at the expense of many others.

This is one place where the Christian community and the institutional Churches can play a vital role. They can offer leadership—not of the political kind but of the inspirational kind. They can challenge people to believe in 'the impossible dream'—and to commit themselves to bringing it about. To take on this task is not an optional extra which Christians and Church leaders are free to choose or ignore. It lies at the heart of the mission of the Church, the mission of bringing salvation to the world. It is the translation into the reality of our world of the Good News which is the Christian message.

The official Church, like other institutions, is somewhat unwieldy. And its leaders are, understandably, chosen more for their wisdom, their humanity and their administrative ability than for their imagination and creativity. So, if the Church is to offer the kind of inspiration which is needed, it needs to make full use of all available resources to help it provide a more creative style of leadership.

God has given some special means or instruments to the Church, to help it develop this kind of leadership. The first such instrument is the prophetic figure—people like Dorothy Day, Helder Camara, Martin Luther King, Pope John XXIII, Dorothee Sölle, Oscar Romero, Ernst Schumacher, Julius Nyerere, Rosemary Haughton, Pedro Arrupe, Gustavo Gutiérrez, Jesse Jackson, and Dan Berrigan. These are successors to the prophets of old; and some of them meet the same fate. But before or after they get martyred (in some degree) they inspire us to believe that what seemed unrealistic or even impossible is not necessarily so. Other ways of doing things are conceivable and it can be a worthwhile Christian venture to devote one's life to showing that a more just and humane way of life is viable.

A second instrument which God has given to the Church for the promotion of inspirational leadership is the communal discernment process. Amazing things happen when Church leaders or committed Christians at any level engage in an unhindered process of discerning—reading the signs of the times and listening for the voice of the Spirit. What comes out of such gatherings may be much more radical than the average opinions of those who went in. Catholics saw this happen at Vatican II and in the 1971 Synod. It happened at Medellín and more recently in the drafting of the joint pastoral letters of the bishops of the United States. Other Christian Churches had similar experiences: one thinks of the first WCC Assembly in Amsterdam in 1948 and the new initiatives that came after, and out of, the Fourth Assembly in 1968 at Uppsala. In all the Churches, many religious organisations, societies, or congregations have experienced it in their own gatherings or assemblies.

A further providential instrument of good leadership in the Church is a committed and highly skilled team of facilitators. What I have in mind is a mixed group of women and men, of lay people and clergy and members of religious communities. This group will have learned (preferably together) the skills of listening to ordinary people and of helping them to articulate their hopes and difficulties. They will have experience of helping people to analysis their situation and of facilitating them as they focus on specific issues. They will be willing to spend time with local people in the careful planning of a programme of action. Such a team can play a key role in breaking through the paralysis which often afflicts Church agencies because of inadequate leadership. It can help the Christian community to bypass or even dismantle the clericalism and authoritarianism which so often arise when Church leaders feel insecure and threatened.

As Christians we can be sure that God will continue to send us prophets to challenge us in our complacency and to comfort us in our trials. But we must work to ensure that our Churches and Church organisations make more effective use of communal discernment and team ministry to enable us to hear the word of God spoken through the voices and lives of prophets. This applies to many areas of life but above all, perhaps, to the difficult task of adopting an alternative set of ideals for human progress and working out a practical alternative model of human development through which these ideals can be put into effect.

Notes

Chapter 1, pp. 7-41.

1. For a clear and comprehensive account of the question of international debt see: George Ann Potter, *Dialogue on Debt: Alternative Analyses and Solutions*, Washington D.C. (Center of Concern: 1988).
2. Quoted in Joe Mihevc, 'Interpreting the Debt Crisis', The Ecumenist, 28 (Nov.-Dec. 1989), 6. For a thorough survey of the economic and moral dimensions of the debt crisis—and some very practical illustrations of its effect on the poor of the Third World— see Seán McDonagh, *The Greening of the Church*, London (Chapman: 1990) and Maryknoll (Orbis: 1990), 9-37; McDonagh's account is particularly effective in bringing out the close link between the debt crisis and the ecological crisis.
3. See my treatment of this question in Donal Dorr, *Integral Spirituality: Resources for Community, Justice, Peace and the Earth*, Dublin (Gill and Macmillan) and Maryknoll (Orbis) 1990, 164-7.

Chapter 2, pp. 45-62.

1. For a detailed account of the development of Vatican social teaching up to 1983 see Donal Dorr, *Option for the Poor: A Hundred Years of Vatican Social Teaching*, Dublin (Gill and Macmillan) and Maryknoll (Orbis), 1983.
2. Cf. Peter Hebblethwaite, *John XXIII: Pope of the Council*, London (Chapman: 1984), especially 325-40.
3. Cf. Dorr, op. cit., 120-38.
4. See, for instance, Gustavo Gutiérrez, *We Drink from Our Own Wells: the Spiritual Journey of a People*, Maryknoll (Orbis: 1984); and *On Job: God-Talk and the Suffering of the Innocent*, Maryknoll (Orbis: 1987); Segundo Galilea, *The Beatitudes: To Evangelize as Jesus Did*, Maryknoll (Orbis: 1984).
5. See my treatment of these four documents in Dorr, op. cit. 139-206.
6. Ibid., 161.
7. See especially his first encyclical, *Redemptor Hominis* ('The Redeemer of Humankind') issued in 1979.
8. See especially the encyclical *Solicitudo Rei Socialis* ('On Social Concern') dated 30 December 1987, but actually issued in 1988. On this point see Donal Dorr, 'Solidarity and Integral Human Development' in Gregory Baum (ed.), *The Logic of Solidarity*, Maryknoll (Orbis: 1990), 143-54.

9. *Laborem Exercens* (translated as 'On Human Work' or as 'On Human Labor') 1981. For an analysis see Gregory Baum, *The Priority of Labor: A Commentary on 'Laborem Exercens', Encyclical Letter of Pope John Paul II*, New York (Paulist: 1982); see also Donal Dorr, *Option for the Poor*, 233-51.
10. Apostolic letter *Dignitate Mulieris*, nos 7, 10, 24-5.
11. 'Peace with God the Creator: Peace with All of Creation', Rome, 8 Dec. 1989. References given are to the numbered paragraphs.
12. Implicit in what I am saying here is a distinction between morality and religion. I understand morality to be based on our obligation to respect fundamental values *within* the world. Consequently, the call to obey God would be a matter of *religion* rather than of morality in the strict sense.
13. Cf. Alan Geyer, 'Two Peace Pastorals Compared', *The Ecumenist*, 28, 1 (Nov.-Dec. 1989), 3.

Chapter 3, pp. 63-82.
1. For a more extensive account see: Paul Bock, *In Search of a Responsible World Society: The Social Teachings of the World Council of Churches*, Philadelphia (Westminster Press: 1974); Edward Duff, *The Social Thought of the World Council of Churches*, London and New York (Longmans, Green and Co: 1956); John Desrochers, *The Social Teaching of the Church*, Bangalore (John Desrochers: 1982); and sundry articles in *The Ecumenical Review*, vol. 40 no. 2 (April 1988).
   I am grateful to Rev. Alan Faulkner, of The Irish School of Ecumenics, for valuable criticism and advice in the writing of this chapter; also to Dr Robert MacAfee Brown for advice about sources.
2. *The Kairos Document: Challenge to the Church: A Theological Comment on the Political Crisis in South Africa* (revised 2nd edition), issued by the Institute of Contextual Theology on behalf of the Kairos theologians, Braamfontein, South Africa, Grand Rapids (Eerdmans) and London (CHR) 1986 (the first edition was published in 1985). Also in 1986 a group calling themselves 'Concerned Evangelicals' issued a response to *The Kairos Document*, entitled *Evangelical Witness in South Africa* (Regnum Books, Oxford), in which they challenge 'the blasphemous preamble' of the present South African constitution. The 'Kairos' inspiration was carried a step further in 1989 by a document signed by Christians from seven Third World nations—*The Road to Damascus: Kairos and Conversion* (Institute of Contextual Theology and Skotaville Publishers, Johannesburg, 1989—and publishers in five other countries). This statement roundly condemns those who use

187

Christianity in an ideological way to lend an appearance of legitimacy to oppression.

3. Geneva (WCC Publications: 1987). (The original German edition was published in 1986).
4. Paul Abrecht, 'From Oxford to Vancouver: Lessons from Fifty Years of Ecumenical Work for Economic and Social Justice', *The Ecumenical Review*, vol. 40, 150.
5. Cf. John C. Bennett, 'Breakthrough in Ecumenical Social Ethics: The Legacy of the Oxford Conference on Church, Community, and State (1937)', *The Ecumenical Review* vol. 40, 144-5.
6. Ibid., 142.
7. Cf. Bock, op. cit., 41.
8. Duff, op. cit., 45.
9. Cf. Bock, op. cit., 129.
10. Cf. Desrochers, op. cit., 474.
11. Cf. Paul Abrecht, art. cit., 160.
12. See Alan Geyer, 'Two Peace Pastorals Compared', *The Ecumenist*, 28, 1 (Nov.-Dec. 1989), 1-4.
13. *Peace with Justice: The official documentation of the European Ecumenical Assembly, Basel, Switzerland, 15-21 May, 1989*, Geneva (Conference of European Churches; 1989), 33-65. (References are given according to the paragraph numbers.)
14. *Between the Flood and the Rainbow: Covenanting for JPIC*, (Second Draft Document for the World Convocation on Justice, Peace and the Integrity of Creation, Seoul, Korea, 5-13 March 1990), Geneva (WCC: Christmas 1989).
15. *Justice, Peace, Integrity of Creation: World Convocation, Seoul, Korea, March 6-12, 1990: Final Document* (World Council of Churches, Central Committee 25-30 March 1990, Document no. 19), Geneva (WCC: 1990). As the preface of the document points out, not all of the text carries the same authority. This is because the available time permitted only some parts of it to be debated and adopted by the convocation as a whole, while other parts come from drafting groups using the material and recommendations put forward by working groups during the convocation. In my account of the contents of the document I am concentrating on the parts that were debated and adopted by the convocation as a whole.
16. See especially the series of books published by Orbis Books, Maryknoll, containing the papers of EATWOT conferences: Sergio Torres and Virginia Fabella, eds, *The Emergent Gospel*, (1977); K. Appiah-Kubi and S. Torres, eds, *African Theology en Route* (1979); V. Fabella, ed., *Asia's Struggle for Full Humanity* (1980); S. Torres and John Eagleson, eds, *The Challenge of Basic Christian Communities* (1981); V. Fabella and S. Torres, eds, *Irruption of the Third World* (1983); V. Fabella and S. Torres, eds, *Doing Theology in a Divided World* (1985).

Chapter 4, pp. 83-102.

1. On the principle of subsidiarity see E. F. Schumacher, *Small is Beautiful: A Study of Economics as if People Mattered*, London (Abacus: 1974), 203-5, and New York (Harper and Row: 1989).

2. I am thinking here of the defence of the notion of the integrity of creation put forward both in the 1990 WCC document from Seoul (which I dealt with in chapter 3 above) and in Pope John Paul's message for the 1990 World Day of Peace (which I dealt with in chapter 2 above). In regard to the sphere of the constitutional laws of nations, weighty arguments have been put forward by respected authorities for giving rights to species, life systems, and distinctive natural features; and there are some precedents for doing so—see Richard Cartwright Austin, *Reclaiming America: Restoring Nature to Culture*, Abingdon, Virginia (Creekside Press: 1990), 162-9.

3. There is a basis for such a theology in the well-known biblical text: 'You must not muzzle an ox when it is treading out the corn.' (Deut 25:4); also in the text that insists on a time of rest for the ox and the donkey (Deut 23:12). Concern for the welfare of wild animals is shown in the text prescribing that they be allowed to feed on fallow land (Ex 23:11).

Chapter 5, pp. 105-25.

1. A different version of some of the following material on option for the poor is to appear in my article in Judith A. Dwyer, ed., *The New Dictionary of Catholic Social Thought*, Collegeville (The Liturgical Press).

2. See, Louis J. Puhl, *The Spiritual Exercises of St Ignatius: based on studies in the language of the autograph*, Chicago (Loyola University Press: 1951, 60-62 (paras 136-46).

3. I owe this insight to a South African Dominican member of a group which was discussing the spirituality of liberation with Albert Nolan in London, under the auspices of the Catholic Institute of International Relations (CIIR). I am unable to recall his name.

4. See Donal Dorr, *Spirituality and Justice*, Dublin (Gill and Macmillan) and Maryknoll (Orbis) 1984, 74-86.

5. For a detailed account of the overall psycho-social method see the three-volume handbook by Anne Hope and Sally Timmel, *Training for Transformation: A Handbook for Community Workers*, Gweru, Zimbabwe (Mambo Press: 1984). Pp. 35-44 of vol. 1 gives an account of the listening survey. In a previous book I described a somewhat different point of entry inspired by the same general philosophy and methodology; the approach which I suggest there puts rather more emphasis on the local culture and for that reason it may prove helpful to people working in areas where there is a sharp contrast

189

between the 'traditional' and the 'modern' patterns of life. See Donal Dorr, *Integral Spirituality: Resources for Community, Justice, Peace, and the Earth*, Dublin (Gill and Macmillan) and Maryknoll (Orbis) 1990, 149–83.

6. *The Road to Damascus: Kairos and Conversion* (Institute of Contextual Theology and Skotaville Publishers, Johannesburg, 1989—and publishers in five other countries), 7.

7. See Thomas Berry, *The Dream of the Earth*, San Francisco (Sierra Club Books: 1988); also Seán McDonagh, *To Care for the Earth: a Call to a New Theology*, London (Chapman: 1986); see also chapter 1 of Donal Dorr, *Integral Spirituality*, op.cit.

8. See Richard Cartwright Austin, *Reclaiming America: Restoring Nature to Culture (Environmental Theology, Book 4)*, Abingdon, Virginia (Creekside Press: 1990), 78–84, 143.

Chapter 6, pp. 126-43.

1. The text is given in *IFDA Dossier*, nos. 75/6 (Jan./Apr. 1990) 45–50.

2. See, for instance, Charlene Spretnak and Fritjof Capra, *Green Politics*, New York (E.P. Dutton: 1984) and London (Paladin, Grafton, Collins: 1985)—written for an American audience about the German Greens mainly: Peter Bunyard and Fern Morgan-Grenville, eds in association with ECOROPA, *The Green Alternative: Guide to Good Living*, London (Methuen: 1987)— mainly about Green policies in Britain; John Gormley, *The Green Guide for Ireland*, Dublin (Wolfhound Press: 1990); Aibhlín McCrann, *Green White and Green: A Green Consumer Guide for Ireland*, Swords, Co. Dublin (Poolbeg Press: 1990).

3. See especially chapter 5 of Donal Dorr, *Integral Spirituality: Resources for Community, Justice, Peace, and the Earth*, Dublin (Gill and Macmillan) and Maryknoll (Orbis) 1990.

4. Other names suggested include 'affection economy', 'survival economy' and 'reciprocity economy'. These names do not seem to be fully accurate since the activities in question may not always be motivated by affection or survival, and there may not always be an element of reciprocity in them. I am indebted to Phillippe Fanchette of the Adult Education section of WCC for much of what I have written about the exchange and the non-exchange economy; but I am aware that my account is grossly over-simplified. Further stimulating ideas about the real nature of the economy and of human development may be found in *Development Dialogue*, 1989:1 (Dag Hammarksjold Foundation, Uppsala).

5. *Integral Spirituality*, chapters 1 and 6.

6. The address of IFDA is: 4 place du marché, 1260 NYON, Switzerland.
7. Richard Cartwright Austin, *Reclaiming America: Restoring Nature to Culture*, Abingdon, Virginia (Creekside Press: 1990), 72–8.
8. Ibid., 194–209.
9. An expanded and adapted version of the remaining part of this chapter has appeared in my essay in Enda McDonagh, ed., *Faith and the Hungry Grass: A Mayo Book of Theology*, Blackrock, Co. Dublin (Columba Press: 1990).
10. Naim Ateek, *Justice and Only Justice*, Maryknoll (Orbis: 1989).
11. I am thinking of groups like 'Traidcraft' in the UK and 'Traideireann' in Ireland.

Chapter 7, pp. 144-62.
1. An earlier and more extended version of the first part of this chapter was published in *Studies* vol. 76, no. 301 (Spring 1987). An earlier extended version of the second part of the chapter was published in *Milltown Studies* no. 21 (Spring 1988).
2. *The Kairos Document: Challenge to the Church: A Theological Comment on the Political Crisis in South Africa* (revised 2nd edition), Braamfontein, South Africa (Institute of Contextual Theology); also London (CIIR) and Grand Rapids, (Eerdmans), 1986, 3–16, especially pp. 8 and 10.
3. In an important paper on theological education James Hopewell pointed out that what he called 'the clerical paradigm' had the effect of promoting an individualistic understanding of ministry when the emphasis should instead be on 'the process and quality of the community's own redemptive quest'. See his article 'A Congregational Paradigm for Theological Eduction' in Joseph C. Hough, Jr and Barbara G. Wheeler, eds, *Beyond Clericalism: The Congregation as a Focus for Theological Education*, Atlanta, Georgia (Scholars Press: 1988), 2 3.
4. This point is well brought out by Anne Primavesi and Jennifer Henderson in their book *Our God Has No Favourities: A Liberation Theology of the Eucharist*, Tunbridge Wells, England (Burns & Oates) and San José, California (Resource) 1989. They point out that in North Atlantic countries the theologies of sexism, racism and ecology are often being worked out by an educated laity rather than by clerics. Consequently, 'The clerical interface between the experience of oppression and its expression is done away with. Those oppressed by the structures speak for themselves. . . . Therefore such liberation theologians feel free to address themselves explicitly to oppression within the churches as well as outside them' (p.7).

191

Chapter 8, pp. 163-82.

1. Martin Kennedy, 'Recognizing the laity's role', *Alpha*, vol. 2 no. 1 (18 Jan. 1990), 8 (emphasis added).

2. Cf. Pope John Paul II, *Solicitudo Rei Socialis* (Encyclical letter 'On Social Concern' dated 30 Dec. 1987), Rome (Libraria Editrice Vaticana: 1988), especially nos. 21–4; the link between justice, peace and ecology is a major motif which runs right through the documents issued by the ecumenical conferences at Basel (1989) and Seoul (1990)—see chapter 3 above.

3. Marjorie Hewitt Suchocki makes the point that 'field education' for theology students is not valued as highly as it is for students of medicine: indeed it is often considered marginal. See her article, 'Friends in the Family: Church, Seminary, and Theological Education' in Joseph C. Hough, Jr. and Barbara G. Wheeler, eds, *Beyond Clericalism: The Congregation as a Focus for Theological Education*, Atlanta, Georgia (Scholars Press: 1988), 53.

4. In an interesting study of a very active and committed local Church, Don S. Browning notes that the pastoral care given by the minister is only a small part of the total care given in the congregation; in fact the minister spends more time in *facilitating* the patterns of care that emerge in a healthy congregation than in giving individual counselling. See his article 'Pastoral Care and the Study of the Congregation' in Hough and Wheeler, op. cit., 107–8. This supports the point I am making that even leading members of a pastoral team may be absent occasionally. Such absence may help others to discover and use their gifts.

5. Donal Dorr, *Integral Spirituality: Resources for Community, Justice, Peace, and the Earth*, Dublin (Gill and Macmillan) and Maryknoll (Orbis) 1990. A more extensive and practically-oriented programme is contained in Anne Hope and Sally Timmel, *Training for Transformation: A Handbook for Community Workers*, Gweru, Zimbabwe (Mambo Press: 1984).

Index

197

scientists, 30–32, 66, 67, 115, 131
Scripture *see* Bible
security forces, 14, 108, 153
sedition, 98
Seoul *see* WCC Assemblies
sexism, 24, 79
sexual discrimination, 22, 23
sexuality, 79, 155
shalom, 75, 123
'Shining Path', 19
sin and grace, 106
social:
  analysis, 13, 113–17
  ethics, 58, 65, 66
  injustice, 8, 14, 24, 118
  issues, 35, 45, 46, 64–7, 72, 74, 117
  justice, 7–11, 18, 22, 25–8, 30, 39–41, 45–82, 105, 117, 119, 125, 126
  justice agenda *see* (social) justice
  security, 29, 36, 48
Social Gospel Movement, 64
socialism, 39, 47, 49–51, 64, 67, 71, 85
society, structures of, 27, 28, 35, 94, 108, 125, 126
socio-economic patterns, 114
solidarity:
  economy of, 130–32
  virtue of, 110
  with the poor, 54, 56, 112, 118, 173
Solidarity, Poland, 94
South, the *see* developing countries
South Africa, 19, 20, 24
Spain, 25, 53
spirituality, 22, 39, 45, 55–6, 80–82, 123–4, 126, 146–51, 153–5, 157, 162, 163, 166, 169, 175, 179
State:
  absolutism, 47, 84, 88
  and Church, 49, 55, 63, 65, 66, 70, 118
  and social security, 8, 29, 36, 51, 95
  and war, 18, 68, 71, 97–9

authority of, 39, 87–90
bureaucracy, 92, 134
other references, 85, 93
strikes, 15, 17, 19, 28, 94, 147
structures:
  alternative, 106–8, 111–13
  economic, 24, 27, 28, 35, 79
  of society, 27, 28, 35, 94, 108, 125, 126, 153
  participative, 15
  political, 36
  other references, 10, 15, 40, 41, 47, 73, 94, 144, 152
subsidiarity, 88, 89, 92
Sudan, 33
super-powers, 14
supply and demand, 34, 64, 96
Synod of Bishops 1971, 40, 57

taxes, taxation, 111, 129, 133, 134, 136
technology, 8, 10, 14, 29–35 passim, 75, 78, 89, 96, 127, 135
Temple, William, 65, 138
terrorism, 151
theologians, 20, 46, 47, 49, 53, 55, 64–7, 70, 72, 82, 87, 99–102, 106, 108, 120–23, 138, 146–7, 149–51, 155–62
theological education, 77, 158–62, 177
theology, 22, 48, 52–61, 66, 68, 72, 79, 81, 82, 97, 113, 121, 123, 144–50, 154–8, 160, 162, 166, 178–80
Third World *see* developing countries
Tibet, 14
torture, 14, 108, 140
trade unions, 20, 64, 94, 129, 137
Travellers, 25
  see also minorities
tribal peoples *see* minorities
Trócaire, 117
tropical forests *see* deforestation
Tutu, Desmond, 73, 120
Two Thirds World, 75
tyranny, 20, 99

UN (United Nations), 21, 26, 88
under-developed *see* developing
under-privileged *see* poor
unemployment, 34–7, 96, 124, 125, 128, 135, 136, 151, 152
United Methodist Council of Bishops, USA, 74
Universal Declaration of Human Rights, 26
Uppsala *see* WCC Assemblies
USA *see* America
USSR, 69
usury *see* interest rates

values, 15, 17, 18, 37–9, 48, 49, 67, 68, 75, 78, 82, 83, 88, 89, 91, 93, 115, 118, 121, 130, 132, 137, 145–7, 149–51, 155–7, 166, 173, 175, 182
Vancouver *see* WCC Assemblies
Vatican, 41, 49, 51, 56, 59, 60, 61, 67, 71, 72, 77, 80
Vatican documents:
    'Church in the Modern World' (Gaudium et Spes), 52, 53, 55, 70, 97, 100
    'Dignity of women' (*Dignitate Mulieris*), 59 n10
    'Evangelisation in the Modern World' (*Evangelii Nuntiandi*), 58
    'Justice in the World', 40, 57
    on the theology of liberation, 59
    Octogesima Adveniens, 57, 69
    'Peace with God the Creator', 60 n11
Vatican Justice and Peace Office, 52
Vatican II, 46, 50, 52–6, 67, 70, 71, 97, 100, 149, 184
violence and non-violence, 18, 20, 54, 75, 76, 78, 79, 81, 98, 99, 123, 150
vocational groups *see* corporatism
vocations, 164, 165
voting rights, 22, 24, 26

Wall Street Crash, 48
war:
    between nations, 21, 98
    just, 53, 68, 70, 99
    other references, 9, 19, 33, 53, 68, 69, 122, 142, 150
waste of resources, 31–2
WCC (World Council of Churches), 46, 62, 63, 66–74, 77, 78, 82, 112, 120, 121, 184
WCC Assemblies and Conferences:
    Amsterdam, 68, 69, 184
    Canberra, 74, 78
    Evanston, 69
    Geneva, 70, 71
    Nairobi, 70, 72
    New Delhi, 68, 70
    Seoul, 62, 77
    Uppsala, 72, 184
    Vancouver, 73, 78
    Zagorsk, 71
wealth *see* rich, the
weapons:
    immoral, 100
    of mass destruction, 68, 80, 88
    other references, 18, 19, 21, 22, 33, 73, 74, 99
welfare state, 51
West, the, 3, 17, 29, 35, 49, 65, 69, 73, 94, 116, 135
women:
    and men, 41, 60, 79, 84, 161, 178, 184
    and the Church, 62, 75, 76–7, 152–3
    justice for, 22–4, 108, 119–20
    ordination of, 59, 120, 156
    other references, 31, 66, 72, 74, 95, 150, 151
women's liberation, 22, 152–3
work:
    and unemployment, 36, 48, 96, 128
    and women, 95, 120
    for justice, 114, 125, 175